370
158
(Pal)

After The Ark

Religious understandings
of ourselves and other

Martin Palmer and Elizabeth Breuilly

fp

FORBES PUBLICATIONS

AFTER THE ARK

© Compassion in World Farming Trust

Published by
Forbes Publications Ltd
Inigo House, 29 Bedford Street, London WC2E 9ED
Tel: 0171 379 1299 Fax: 0171 379 6740

All rights reserved
First published 1996
ISBN 1 899527 03 6

Martin Palmer and Elizabeth Breuilly have asserted their right under the Copyright, Designs and Patents Act 1988 to be identified as the Authors of this Work Copyright materials reproduced in this book are acknowledged on p.92

Printed in Great Britian

Contents

Introduction

This book was commissioned by Compassion in World Farming Trust, the educational wing of Compassion in World Farming, an organisation which campaigns for the humane treatment of farm animals. *After the Ark* does not advocate or endorse the particular views of CIWF - rather it endorses the importance of these issues.

CIWF's concern is to give teachers the opportunity, and the necessary material, to raise these issues in Religious Education and related lessons at key stage 3. But as we worked on the book in a series of working parties with CIWF and consultants from different faiths, we realised that the issues of the treatment of farm animals actually express much deeper attitudes about the natural world, and particularly about the relationship between humanity and the rest of the animal world. It is not sufficient to say that all religions tell us to treat animals with compassion. The reasons underlying that compassion, and the perception of animals and humanity which it embodies, vary enormously from one religion to another. This book explores those differences, and invites each reader to explore, express, and possibly modify his or her own view.

In writing the book, we drew on the experience and methods of our previous education books for this age group, *Worlds of Difference* (Blackie, 1985), which first made a link between religion and ecology, and *Religion for a Change*, (Stanley Thornes 1991), which uses story, both contemporary and traditional, to explore issues in religion.

This book encourages both students and teacher to think, to discuss, to disagree, and to decide for themselves. We present to young people some of the issues involved in our treatment of animals, together with the insights which many of the major world faiths have into animals and our relationship with them, but in a way that does not preach or present easy answers.

Why use this book?

The treatment of animals is a subject which tends to arouse strong feelings, especially in young people. It raises many issues of right and wrong, rights and duties, and of personal choices which students are keen to grapple with. At the same time, Religious Education and PSE often have to work hard to show students their relevance to anything which interests them. Our approach sets out a clear course of study for students to get to grips with an important issue, while at the same time it increases their knowledge and understanding of religious thought by looking at what the world's faiths have to say on the subject.

Who is it for?

The book is designed for both teachers and students. The teacher will find ideas in RE, PSRE or Humanities, for:

- classroom sessions
- discussion activities
- longer projects
- homework
- assembly ideas based on each chapter of the book, which can be used in conjunction with classroom work or, in some cases, as stand-alone, off-the-shelf assemblies.

Students will find source material and ideas for project work and discussion. Those who are already concerned about the methods used in today's food production and in current eating habits will find information and arguments to support their case. Those who believe that human needs are paramount and see no problem in the way animals are treated will have plenty of opportunity to argue their case.

How to use this book

This book is designed to be used in a variety of ways.

- It can be used as a full course for a term's RE or PSRE. The chapters explore many aspects of humanity's relationship with animals in a logical progression, giving insights from religions where relevant, and opportunities to discuss important questions. The assemblies could be used to add value to this course of study.

- It can be used as a teacher's resource to add an extra dimension to various subjects covered in RE. For example, the question of rights and duties is here first discussed in a fairly general way, then applied to the question of animal rights. This specific focus could be used as one aspect of a more wide-ranging discussion of rights. In the same way, the chapter, 'Do all animals deserve the same?' can be used in a discussion of discrimination. In covering these subjects, the students will be introduced to a wide range of religious knowledge and religious concepts from major world faiths.

- It can be used as a source book for assemblies. Many of the assemblies can be used in isolation from the course as a whole, and many of the extracts from religious writings which appear throughout the book can be used as readings in assembly.

- It can be used as a resource for individual project work by students. 'Animals', 'animal rights', 'cruelty to animals' and related subjects are often suggested by students as chosen subjects for a project, and students will find assembled in this book a variety of factual and religious material on these subjects, as well as suggested research projects which could lead them well beyond a simple 'be nice to animals' message.

Structure of the book

Each chapter contains stories, information, scriptural passages and activities. Some of the stories are traditional ones from different faiths. Others follow the activities, discussions and difficulties of a group of young people as they encounter different aspects of the topic. The activities have been designed for a variety of abilities, as well as variations in the time available.

We felt it important to 'begin at the beginning', almost literally, so the first chapter looks at creation stories. Without some idea of the variety of ways in which people think about the beginning of the world, the creation or evolution of all that exists, it is impossible to get to grips with different views about the relationships between different creatures.

Chapters 2 and 3 focus respectively on humanity and the rest of the animal world, in each case asking the questions 'What kind of creature is this? What is it for?'. Both these chapters begin to explore the relationship between humans and animals, each from a different perspective.

Chapters 4, 5, 6 and 7 then focus on particular issues: rights and duties, discrimination, science and technology, and death. In each case, we give a brief overview of the whole question, and some of the broad areas of discussion which arise in connection with it. We then focus more specifically on the treatment of animals in general, and farm animals in particular.

At various points in these chapters, reference is made to the last two chapters, Farming Information' and 'Action'. We had two reasons for not including information and suggestions for action within each chapter:
(i) Reference to the same information or possible action is often made from several different places in chapters 4-7, and these are easier to find when grouped in one chapter.
(ii) Some students will have already learnt much of what is contained in Chapter 8 and taken some of the actions suggested in Chapter 9. For many of them this will have been quite a painful process and we feel that if, for example, they do not wish to read the details of the distress suffered by battery chickens, they should have that choice.

The 'Assemblies' chapter gives full plans for seven assemblies with links to the classwork, as well as brief suggestions for presenting assemblies based on further work on the subject.

 **CHAPTER 1**

Some Questions

God only knows — or does he?

There is a very old Indian poem written some three thousand years ago, which discusses the beginnings of the universe. It says that at the very beginning of time there was nothing, just blankness. No air, no sky, no body. 'So what was there?' the poem then asks, 'And who was there looking after it?' In this nothing, says the poem, a breath stirred. But what breath? Where from? Love began, but from whom, by whom?

'But who really knows?
Who can tell -
How it was born,
where creation began?'

Many people's answer would be that it was God who began the universe, but the poem, called the *Rig Veda Creation Hymn*, finally ends:

'He (God) only knows.
Or, He too knows it not!'

Have you ever thought about where everything came from or about why we are here?

For thousands of years people have asked questions about where life has come from and how it began. And often, as in the *Rig Veda Creation Hymn*, they have finished with a question or a 'perhaps, perhaps not'.

Today we can conjecture about *how* we think things began, but we still have no answer from science as to *why* they began. In earlier times, people took the scientific evidence that they had and tried to work out both how and why all things came to be as they are.

In the first book of the Bible called 'Genesis' (which means beginning), there are descriptions or accounts of the start of creation. For Christians and Jews these descriptions are helpful in giving some idea of how and why the universe began. But they raise just the same sort of questions as the Indian poem does.

i Scientific Theories of the Origins of the Universe

There is still much debate about how the universe and life on earth began and developed. Many scientists believe that the 'big bang' is the best account so far of the origins of the universe. It seems as if between 15,000 and 20,000 million years ago the universe began as an incredibly dense (4,000 million times that of water) and incredibly hot (100,000 million degrees C.) mixture of sub-atomic particles. This then expanded very rapidly, and larger particles were formed, to form first atoms and then molecules. These group into stars and galaxies, and planets, such as our earth, that circulate round stars.

Life on earth is believed to have started when certain gases combined together under the influence of ultra-violet light and electrical energy such as lightning. These formed amino-acids, which in turn can combine to form proteins. Some experiments have gone some way to show how DNA could also have arisen in the conditions on earth millions of years ago. The beginning of DNA is important because it is able to reproduce itself and give instructions for the forming of proteins from amino-acids. This means that cells can grow and reproduce - they have life.

The forms of life on earth are believed to have developed in response to changing conditions on earth. Those that could best adapt to the conditions survived and reproduced.

Activities

1. Brainstorm in class on the question 'What is there in the universe?' and write down all the answers suggested. In order to keep the list to a reasonable length, use categories, e.g. trees, plants, land animals, fish, insects, land, water, planets, stars, space, etc.
Do you think it is possible to find a theory or account which describes how they all came into being?

2. Read Genesis chapter 1 to chapter 2, verse 3. This account gives a general order in which parts of the universe were created. For the moment, ignore the fact that it is pictured in terms of 'days'. Make a chart as shown and write in all the categories you wrote down in question 1 at the appropriate stage when the Bible says they were created.

Stage 1	
Stage 2	
Stage 3	
Stage 4	
Stage 5	
Stage 6	

3. Look at the box on the scientific account of the beginnings of the universe. Make a new table like the one above, with as many stages as you think are necessary. Arrange the list from question 1 into stages as you did before, this time using the scientific account.

4. Compare the two tables. What are the differences? Were there some parts of the universe which you found difficult to fit into either of the tables?

More questions than answers

The Jews have a tradition that no one should be allowed to read the first two chapters of the Book of Genesis without a teacher or companion. There are so many unanswered and unanswerable questions in those two chapters, that you could go mad trying to make sense of it by yourself!

Today people use many different ideas to form their vision of how, and more importantly, why the universe exists. Most scientific accounts do not claim to answer the question 'why' and scientists disagree about what exactly our scientific information does or does not tell us about how the universe began. But best-seller lists are full of books which speculate on why. It seems we really want an answer! Three thousand years on from the Indian poem quoted earlier and we are still asking the same questions and still arriving at the same uncertainty.

It seems we keep asking because we want to have some sort of feeling that we understand creation and our role in it. If we really just thought of ourselves as totally unimportant blobs of life, on an unimportant planet, on the edge of a not very important galaxy somewhere in space, we would find it difficult to know how to live our lives - we have to believe that something matters! As it is, we all have some sort of story or stories in our heads which make us feel that not only is our planet important and not only is our species important, but we, individually, are important.

Activities

1. For thousands of years people have tried to find answers but have ended up with more questions. Try writing your own 'creation' poem including your theories and your questions about where and how everything began. You may have religious or scientific ideas you want to put in, but think carefully and be honest about which questions they answer and which ones remain unanswered.

2. Read the descriptions of creation in Genesis chapter 1 and 2. Using your own poem and the Indian poem, see what questions the Genesis account leaves unanswered, and see which ones are still for you unanswerable.

Of Humans and Dinosaurs

Mr Coustin had at last got his act together and arranged for the class to visit the local museum. For many it was their first time inside the old building with its rather formal entrance. In the entrance hall there was an enormous model dinosaur on display.

"Makes you think, doesn't it" said Joseph. "They used to run the world. The most important species for twenty or thirty million years and now they're extinct. Brain the size of a pea, it's not surprising".

"So how come you're not extinct then?" quipped Michelle.

"Oh very funny" replied Joseph. "No, what I mean is, they had to die out so we could come along with our more powerful brains. It's all part of the progress of evolution isn't it - more primitive creatures give way to better ones."

"Do you really think evolution is progressive?" asked Pallavi. "I'm not at all sure that it is."

"What do you mean?" asked Joseph. "Stands to reason its progressive. Look at us. We're the most highly evolved species, kind of top of the tree. We can read and write, invent things, control things. Even human beings are getting better and cleverer over time. Just look at what things were like only fifty years ago."

Joseph spotted another exhibition. It was about the Egyptian creation stories and the poster for it showed an ancient Egyptian painting of the sky as a man and the earth as a woman.

"See. Look at that. We don't believe stories like that any more do we? See how we have improved since ancient Egyptian times."

"Well, I'm not so sure" said Pallavi. "See, I think that life goes more in kinds of cycles. We have tens of thousands of lives, as different creatures. For me, this is just one of any number of reincarnations. I don't think human beings are that special. And who says the Egyptians were wrong? Their world view of the earth as a Mother is just like some forms of Hinduism, who treat the world in a gentle way because they think it is a Mother to us. I think that is actually more civilised than what most of us do!"

"Do you really believe that every creature is just the same kind of soul but in a different body?' asked Christine.

"Yes, I do" replied Pallavi, "so maybe, once upon a time, you were a dinosaur, Joseph."

"And next time round he'll be a rat", joked Gavin.

"Look you lot, take this seriously will you" said Christine. "Do you mean Pallavi, that nothing really progresses? I don't believe in God or gods or any of that stuff, but I do sometimes wonder why we're here. I suppose that was what the Egyptians were trying to deal with in their creation stories. What all creation stories sort of deal with. I don't need that sort of story but I can see the basic question. I mean, it's why us, now?"

"Well" said Pallavi, "I believe we are what we are because of what we did in the past. So, say Joseph did live like a rat, trying to get everything for himself, destroying what he couldn't get, then he might be reborn as a rat next time."

"I don't believe that," said Michelle. "I think we have one life and God wants us to do the best we can with it. He created human beings and he created rats and he put each animal in its place. And humans have a special place, we're the most important, aren't we Gavin?"

Gavin had been engrossed in looking at the display of a Stone Age burial and hadn't been paying much attention. "You what?" he said vaguely.

"The question being addressed" said Christine who always sounded as if she was giving a lecture, "is why are we here?"

"Cos Mr Coustin managed to get the school bus!" said Gavin.

"Very funny" said Christine. "You know what I mean. Where have we come from, where are we going, why are human beings so powerful, why did the dinosaurs die out? You know, simple basic questions like that Gavin."

"Yes, like why did City get relegated last year?" said Joseph.

"No, come on," interrupted Leila, "These are good questions. How do you all set about answering them?"

"Why are we here?" asked Gavin. "Well, God made us and gave us the earth to live in. We can use it and enjoy it, but it isn't ours. We're like caretakers I suppose, but we are allowed to party as well!"

"So does this give you the right to use anything?", asked Pallavi. "Like, does it mean you think you have rights over everything else?"

"No" said Leila, "we don't exactly have rights. God is the real ruler, and we rule on his behalf - he's given us the authority to do it. It's called "Khalifa" in Arabic -it means something like "vice-regent""

"Oh yes", said Joseph, "Our rabbi was going on about something like that a few weeks ago. He said something about us being here to enjoy everything God has given, but to also make sure that we don't destroy anything that God has made."

"But how can you do that?" retorted Christine. "Look around you. Humans destroy something every time they do anything. They destroy rainforests, they destroyed that park down the road by building on it - people needed houses, I know it had to be done, but something's gone that won't ever come back. We need to get rid of all this religion stuff and just work out proper economic, social and political programmes to use the world properly."

"Fine" said Leila, "But who decides what is the 'best use'? Ask the head of any government what is 'best' and I bet their ideas would differ from your ideas! If we just go on human ideas we'll end up fighting. We Muslims believe that we need God to tell us what is right and he has given us the guidance we need in the Qur'an. If we don't follow it we'll just make a mess of things."

"That's right!" said Michelle. "You know I'm not a Muslim, but I know that God will judge us all in the end. I know that when I face Jesus on the last day, I must be able to show I have lived according to His Will."

"Yes, but I don't believe it should be fear of the Final Day that makes you want to act properly," said Gavin.

"Well, what will?" asked Christine, "I suppose you're going to say love, or something like that. But love hasn't done much for us so far, has it? Just look at what human beings are doing to the world, to each other and to other creatures. What makes us think we are the top species?"

"I don't think we're the top, exactly ...", said Gavin. But the discussion was cut short by a loud shout from the one person they all recognised as being on top, a very cross Mr Coustin who had come back to see where the six of them had got to!

Activities

1. Joseph says that human beings are getting cleverer and better over time. Does Pallavi agree with him? Describe Pallavi's opinion in your own words.

2. Christine says she can 'see the basic question'. In the conversation that follows, different people put forward different ideas. Look at the story and write down three different questions that any of the group ask, which they feel are important and basic.
If you think that someone is asking a question that is not expressed clearly, you can put it into your own words.

3. Joseph thought that the world in general, and humanity in particular, has been getting better as time goes on. Ask a number of older people what they think has got better in the world in their lifetime and what they think has got worse. Compare all your lists. Overall, does it seem that most people think the world is getting better or worse? Do you agree?

4. Imagine the world in fifty years time. What do you hope will be better, what do you fear will be worse? Draw a picture of the world as you think it might be. Will there be room for plants, trees and animals?

CHAPTER 2

Humanity - Are We So Special?

Are we the most important part of the universe?

Would the planet be better off without us?

In all creation stories, whether they be ancient or modern (like the various scientific stories), the role of human beings always raises questions. Even if you do not believe in a creator, or in a creative process as such, the place of humans needs some explanation. In all the stories, it seems that human beings end up in the centre of the stage. Perhaps this is because it is human beings who tell the stories.

But why are we here? What is the role of our species? Does everything else exist just for us to use? And what sort of relationship should we have with the rest of creation? These are some of the questions we explore in this second chapter. We are using the word 'creation' to mean 'everything that exists' - it is up to you to decide what you think that means and how you think it came to exist!

Why Did it Take so Long?

By the time lunchtime came, the group of friends were worn out. If they had to look at another bone or fossil they thought they would die!

Gratefully, they found a corner of the Museum school room and sank down to rest.

"I never knew it could take so long to get through evolution", said Pallavi.

"Yep, nearly 600 million years" said Joseph.

"I meant", said Pallavi with a sigh, "I never thought it would take all morning to go through the exhibition."

For a while, there was silence as they began to eat. Then Michelle spoke:

"You know what makes me wonder? Why did it take so long for human beings to be made? I mean, look at all those hundreds of millions of years with just fishes and reptiles and stuff. Makes you wonder what they were there for."

"Well, it takes time for things to reach a stage of perfection" said Joseph.

"Ha!" spluttered Christine, half way through a sandwich. "Typical. What makes you think that human beings are the perfection of evolution anyway? Seems to me there were lots of other creatures which were far more successful than human beings have been. Animals that were perfectly adapted to their environment for hundreds of millions of years. Yet they passed away. If I was judging the most successful species, I don't even think human beings would appear on my list."

"So you think that most of evolution has nothing to do with us?" asked Michelle.

"Yes, obviously" said Christine.

"That's all well and good, but those animals are now extinct and it's human beings who are in control" said Gavin, who then caught the look on Leila's face. "Well, OK, sort of in control, sometimes, maybe. Point is, it looks to me as if we are the most important species and that's that."

"But surely," said Christine "those of you who believe in God can't imagine that He, She or It made everything, over hundreds of millions of years, just for us. Isn't that terribly arrogant? Surely somebody or something actually enjoys creation for its own sake?"

"Fair point" said Pallavi. "I've never thought about it like that, but yes I believe all things are loved for themselves - animals, birds, trees, rocks, plants, even human beings!"

"Well, yes, of course," said Michelle, "but I still think human beings are the most important. God created us to be special."

Before anyone could cut in, Mr Coustin's voice interrupted their thoughts. "Excuse me I'm sure, but you may not have noticed that the more evolutionarily advanced members of your class heard me call everyone to go into the Film Theatre. Perhaps you lesser specimens would care to join us?" The tone of voice indicated that this was not a question they were expected to debate!

Activities

1. In the story, what does Christine think about why the world was created? What does Pallavi think?

2. Imagine that you have been given the power to travel back to a time before human beings existed. You can observe this world, but the animals are unaware of your existence and you cannot affect their lives in any way. Write a story about what you see, hear, smell etc.

3. In groups of three, compare the worlds you have each imagined in activity 2. Discuss in your groups:

a) Is this a world you would like to inhabit? If so, in what form (human or other)?

b) Do any of you feel that there is something important missing in these imagined worlds?

c) Would the imagined world be a better place if there were humans in it? If so, in what ways? If not, why not?

God's View, Ancestor's View

In the past different religions have said, in different ways, "Look, you human beings are not the only important things in creation". Below are two examples, one taken from the Book of Job in the Bible, a story of great importance to both Jews and Christians. It dramatically describes the richness of the natural world and emphasises how little knowledge and control human beings have over it. The other is taken from Australian Aboriginal tradition. It speaks of the immense variety of nature in a rather different way, but with the same enthusiasm and enjoyment.

God's answer to Job

Then the Lord answered Job out of the storm. He said:
'Who is this that darkens my counsel with words without knowledge?
Brace yourself like a man;
I will question you,
and you shall answer me.
Where were you when I laid the earth's foundation?
Tell me, if you understand.
Who marked off its dimensions?
Surely you know!   *Job 38:1-5*

'Have you journeyed to the springs of the sea
or walked in the recesses of the deep?
Have the gates of death been shown to you?
Have you seen the gates of the shadow of death?
Have you comprehended the vast expanses of the earth?
Tell me, if you know all this.   *Job 38:16-18*

'Do you hunt prey for the lioness
and satisfy the hunger of the lions
when they crouch in their dens
or lie in wait in a thicket?
Who provides food for the raven
when its young cry out to God
and wander about for lack of food?
Do you know when the mountain goats give birth?
Do you watch when the doe bears her fawn?
Do you count the months till they bear?
Do you know the time they give birth?
They crouch down and bring forth their young;
their labour pains are ended.

Their young thrive and grow strong in the wilds;
they leave and do not return.
Who let the wild donkey go free?
Who untied his ropes?
I gave him the wasteland for his home,
the salt flats as his habitat.
He laughs at the commotion in the town;
he does not hear a driver's shout.
He ranges the hills for his pasture
and searches for any green thing'.

Job 38:39-39:8

Making the Animals

(Adapted from *A Tapestry of Tales*, Sandra Palmer and Elizabeth Breuilly, Collins Educational, 1993)

A story from the Australian Aborigines.

In the far off time all beings were asleep. No people, animals, birds, grass, trees, streams, rivers were found on the earth. At last the Father of All Spirits awoke the Sun Mother. She looked down on the earth and was sad, for she saw only a bare and empty world. The Father of All Spirits spoke:

"Go down to earth. Cover the ground with grass and trees. Fill the rivers and streams with water. Bring to life all insects and fish and reptiles and birds and animals."

The Sun Mother warmed the earth and the trees and plants sprang up. The animals woke from their cold sleep in a deep cave and came out into the light and warmth. The Sun Mother told them to live together in friendship.

"Enjoy the earth until the day when your bodies will fall asleep and return to dust and your spirits live on to dream unseen until they are again awakened and given new bodies."

For a while all creatures lived peacefully together. Then some became greedy and jealous. The kangaroos wanted to fly, the lizard wanted to swing from the trees, the fish wanted feet to run on the bottom of the sea. More and more they quarrelled until one day Sun Mother left the sky to talk with them.

"My children, why are you so dissatisfied? Choose what kind of living creatures you want to be. One day you may be sorry, but just for today you may have the power to change yourselves into any shape you wish."

What strange creatures emerged! Fish grew wings and appeared to fly. Possums turned into bats. Wallabies climbed trees. Insects looked like twigs. Kangaroos grew a pouch and a tail. Platypus became the strangest creature of all. It had a bill like a duck, it laid eggs, it had teeth to chew with and a beaver's tail. Two feet were webbed like a duck. All four feet had bear's claws and its babies suckled milk from its breast.

The Sun Mother bore two beautiful children; the morning star and the morning. They in turn had two other children. Their grandmother sent them to earth; the first man and the first woman. "My children", she said "live together in peace. You have no need to envy any other living thing and when you die your spirits will live as stars for ever".

The strange creatures all exist in Australia - there is a flying squirrel which resembles both a possum and a bat. There are tree-climbing wallabies, flying fish, stick insects, and, of course, the duck-billed platypus.

Activities

1. The passages from Job describe a world of nature and wild animals which are completely unaffected by human activity and of which humans are largely unaware. (The description continues through several more pages.)
Do you think there is any creature in the world that is unaffected by human activity? (Think about the depths of the sea, the Arctic regions, deserts perhaps.)

2. The passages from Job emphasise how little human beings know about the life of wild animals.
a) Find at least three questions to which the answer must have been 'no', or 'I don't know' when the poem was written.
b) Do you think that the answer would still be the same today, with increased scientific knowledge? Explain your answer.

3. The Aboriginal story is one account of how people and animals came to be. Find out about at least one other story. This might be scientific (try looking in one or more encyclopedias under 'evolution'), or religious (read Genesis chapter 1 in the Bible, or look at the stories in *Worlds of Difference* by Martin Palmer and Esther Bissett, Blackie, 1989), or personal (ask people you know to tell you what they think).
Draw a picture or a diagram to illustrate this story, or tell the story in your own words.

4. Make a collection of all the different stories that the class have found as well as the ideas contained in both the Aboriginal story and the account in Job and in Genesis. Compare the different stories with each other. For each story answer the following questions:
a. Were the world and the animals created by one person?
b. If not, what kind of process created the animals?
c. Do animals change and develop in the story, or do they stay the same all the way through?
d. Were humans and other animals created at the same time?
e. If not, which came first?
f. Is there a reason given for why animals and humans were created?
g. If so, what is the reason?

Humanity — What for?

At different times and in different religions there have been any number of ways of considering the human race. Are we the most important? If so, why? What makes humanity different from animal life? Or is there in fact no real difference? The following passages from the writings of several different faiths give different perspectives on humanity.

From the Bible (used by Jews and Christians):
Then God said, "Let us make man in our image, in our likeness, and let them rule over the fish of the sea and the birds of the air, over the livestock, over all the earth, and over all the creatures that move along the ground."
So God created man in his own image,
in the image of God he created him;
male and female he created them.
God blessed them and said to them, "Be fruitful and increase in number; fill the earth and subdue it. Rule over the fish of the sea and the birds of the air and over every living creature that moves on the ground."
Then God said, "I give you every seed-bearing plant on the face of the whole earth and every tree that has fruit with seed in it. They will be yours for food. And to all the beasts of the earth and all the birds of the air and all the creatures that move on the ground - everything that has the breath of life in it - I give every green plant for food."
And it was so.
And God saw all that he had made, and it was very good.   *Genesis 1:28-31*

When I consider your heavens,
the work of your fingers,
the moon and the stars,
which you have set in place,
What is man that you are mindful of him,
the son of man that you care for him?
You made him a little lower than the heavenly beings
and crowned him with glory and honour.

You made him ruler over the works of your hands;
you put everything under his feet:
all flocks and herds, and the beasts of the field,
the birds of the air, and the fish of the sea,
all that swim in the paths of the seas.

O Lord, our Lord, how majestic is your name in all the earth!   *Psalm 8:3-9*

From the Qur'an
Behold, your Lord said to the Angels: 'I will create a viceregent on earth.' They said: 'Will You place there one who will make mischief there and shed blood, while we celebrate Your praises and glorify Your Holy Name?' He said: 'I know what you do not know.'
And He taught Adam the nature of all things: then he placed them before the Angels and said 'Tell Me the nature of these if you are right.'
They said: 'Glory to You. Of Knowledge, we have none, except what you have taught us: in truth it is You who are perfect in Knowledge and Wisdom.'
He said: 'Adam, tell them their natures.' When he had told them Allah said: 'Did I

not tell you that I know the secrets of the heavens and earth and I know what you reveal and what you conceal?'
Qur'an 2:30-33

From Buddhist writings of Dharmarakshita, *The Wheel of Sharp Weapons*

All of the sufferings that we have endured
In the lives we have led in the three lower states
As well as our pains in the present and future
Are the same as the case of the maker of arrows
Who later was killed by an arrow he had made.
Our suffering is the wheel of sharp weapons returning
Full circle upon us from wrongs we have done
Hereafter let us always have care and awareness
Never to act in non-virtuous ways.

Activities

1. Several of the passages above refer to the power that human beings have. Find as many examples of this as you can. For each of them, write down:
a) what power do we have?
b) are there limits to this power?

2. The passage quoted from the Buddhist writings, instead of looking at the power of human beings, is describing the results of human actions. What does it say will be the result of a bad action?

3. In the previous section on page 10, Joseph said that dinosaurs 'used to run the world' and now it is humans who do that. Do you agree that dinosaurs ran the world? In what sense? Make a list of similarities and differences between the ways in which humans and dinosaurs can be said to 'run the world'. Compare different peoples' lists. Can you make any general statements from this?

CHAPTER 3

Know Your Place

What are animals? Are they beings just like ourselves with feelings, emotions, intelligence and their own relationship with God or the gods? Or are they so much simpler in their bodies and brains than human beings, that we might as well compare them with machines? Why do they exist? Are they in the world to serve our needs?

With some animals we have a very close relationship, sometimes even living with them as members of our family. We use other animals in various ways, such as killing them for food, using substances they produce, training them to work for us, or betting on their skills and strength. Some animals we fear and destroy, others we destroy simply because they are a nuisance, or because they are using land that we want for our own purposes. Why do we admire some animals and despise others? Religions have many different things to say about animals and how we treat them.

Heaven's Provision

A Taoist story from China

Mr T'ien intended going on a long journey. To prepare for this he offered sacrifices to the gods of the road and gave a great feast for a thousand guests. When the dishes of fish and goose were brought round Mr T'ien looked at them happily and said: 'How kind Heaven is to humanity! It provides the five grains and nourishes the fish and birds for us to enjoy and use.'

All the guests agreed; all, that is, except the twelve-year-old son of Mr Pao. He stepped forward and said: 'My Lord is wrong! All life is born in the same way that we are and we are all of the same kind. One species is not nobler than another: it is simply that the strongest and cleverest rule over the weaker and more stupid. Things eat each other and are then eaten, but they were not bred for this. To be sure, we take the things which we can eat and consume them, but you cannot claim that Heaven made them in the first place just for us to eat. After all, the mosquitoes and gnats bite our skin, tigers and wolves eat our flesh. Does this mean Heaven originally created us for the sake of the mosquitoes, gnats, tigers and wolves?'

(Adapted from: Martin Palmer, *The Elements of Taoism*, Element 1992

Activities

1. The story gives two views about the relationship between animals and humans (one from Mr T'ien and one from the twelve-year-old boy). Put each of those views into your own words.

2. There are many other ways of thinking about animals. Choose one of the views listed below and write a dramatic scene expressing that particular view. Your scene could be a discussion between two people, as in the story, or a discussion between a human and an animal. (The animal could be asking, 'Why are you treating me this way?'):

a) humans use animals for research;
b) humans think animals are picturesque or 'sweet';
c) humans ignore animals;
d) humans compare themselves with animals ('brave as a lion').

3. Make a list of expressions and metaphors we use which refer to animals, or make comparisons with animals, for example 'a dog's life', 'pig-ignorant', 'brave as a lion'. Make your own list, and then pool them to form a class list. (The authors found over a hundred in a brief brain-storming session!)

From your list, can you make any general statements about the way we think about animals?

Adam Names the Animals

The ancient Jewish wisdom tells how in the beginning, God created the heavens and the earth, the seas and fishes, the air and the birds, the land and the animals. But none of these creatures had names. Last of all, God created Adam and Eve. All the other creatures had sprung forth from the earth or the sea by God's command, but he moulded Adam and Eve with his own hands.

Then God gathered together all the creatures he had made and told his angels to give them all their proper name. The angels began the task of giving each creature its proper name but they found they could not manage it. They looked at the millions of creatures that God in his wisdom and power had created and they could not find the right name for each one. But Adam spoke up without hesitation:

"O Lord of all the world, King of the Universe, the proper name for this animal is lion, for this one elephant, for this one mouse, for this one dolphin, for this one crab, for this one mosquito..." and so on, until he had given each creature its name. All the names he gave to the creatures were exactly suited to their nature and to the particular skill that God had given them and God was pleased with his naming.

Then God said to Adam, "And you, what is your name?" Adam answered,

"My name is Adam, because you made me out of the dust of the earth, which is called Adamah."

God said to Adam, "And what is my name?"

Adam replied, "You are Adonai, the Lord, because you are Lord over all that you have created, the earth, the heavens, the sea, the sky, over all the creatures and over me and my wife."

God replied, "You are right. The Lord is my name for ever and ever".

_i_   Jewish and Christian view of human authority over animals

In the book of Genesis in the Bible, human beings are described as having authority over animals.

God blessed them and said to them, "Be fruitful and increase in number; fill the earth and subdue it. Rule over the fish of the sea and the birds of the air and over every living creature that moves on the ground." _Genesis 1:28_

Some people have said that 'ruling over' means humans can do what they like with the world and with the animals in it. Others point to the passage in Genesis which says that men and women were made 'in the image of God'. They say that this means that they must act like God and take care of his creation. One word that is frequently used to describe this is 'stewardship'. A steward takes care of a farm or household on behalf of the owner, for the benefit of all who live in it. The steward does not own the property, but has authority and makes decisions.

Islamic Concept of Khalifah

The Qur'an says that human beings are the highest living creature that God created - higher even than the angels. It tells a similar story to the Jewish story above, when the angels could not tell God the nature of the animals he had created, but God had given Adam knowledge that was hidden from the angels. They are told to bow down to Adam, and Adam is described as God's Khalifah - one who rules on behalf of another. The earth and everything in it are God's, but humans have God's authority to rule over it.

In another verse the Qur'an says:
It is He who has made you His agents, inheritors of the earth. _S. 6, verse 165_

So human beings are regarded as having authority and power over animals, and God has given them the sense of right and wrong that will enable them to use this authority on God's behalf. Animals are given to human beings for their use, but there are strict rules about how they are used. We will look at some of these rules later in the book.

Activities

1. In your family, who would have the right to give a name to:
a) a new baby
b) a pet
c) a toy or mascot?
What gives them this right?

2. In the light of your answers to question 1, what do you think the story is implying about the relationship between humans and animals? Read the information boxes about Christian and Jewish teaching about animals and humans to help you answer this.

3. The names that people give to animals and whether they give names at all, often reveal how they think of those animals. In groups, make a list of animals

which might be given names and a list of animals which normally would not. Compare the lists from different groups, and try to decide what makes one list different from another.

Then take your list of animals which might have a name, and suggest suitable names for each species, for example:

cows: Buttercup, Daisy

budgerigar: Joey

Can you make any general comments about the type of names that each species may have?

Australian Aboriginal attitude to animals

The Ancestors of everything that lives in the world today had both a human shape and an animal or plant shape. They travelled across the land hunting and gathering food, camping, having adventures, naming the different species and giving birth. This time of the Ancestors journeys is known as the Dreaming. At the end of their journeys the Ancestors went back into the land or up into the sky and exist still as rocks, rivers, stars and so on. So not only is their spirit all along their journey tracks but they are also physically present in the land.

The Ancestors had many children. Some were human and some were animals or plants. For example, the Rock Wallaby Ancestor is the ancestor to the rock wallaby humans and to the rock wallaby animal. Both are said to have the Ancestral spirit in them.

A species which is a descendant of the same Ancestors as an Aboriginal person is a relative of that person. In this way, Aboriginal families include other species as well as humans.

People with different Ancestors marry one another so through their extended families, Aboriginal people are related to many species that share their territory. The Ancestors gave the land to both their human and non-human descendants and told them how they should relate to one another.

While the Aboriginal people can only survive by eating the species that share the land with them, there are very strict rules as to when they can hunt and gather the different species. This ensures that no species is wiped out. Everyone has at least one nature relative as a totem that must never be harmed or eaten. Usually the totem is inherited through the father in the same way that we inherit our surname through our father.

St Francis and the Birds

(Adapted from the *Little Flowers of St Francis*)

This is how St Francis preached:

'My sisters the birds, you owe much to God your creator and you ought to praise him always and everywhere, because he has given you liberty to fly wherever you wish and has given you clothing with intricate layers. Furthermore, he saved your species on Noah's Ark so that your race was not destroyed. Again, you owe to him the air that he made for you; and you neither sow nor reap, yet God feeds you and gives you rivers and fountains to drink from. He gives you mountains and valleys as a sanctuary for you and high trees to build your nests in. You do not know how to sew or spin, but God clothes you and your little ones. Your Creator shows you how much he loves you by giving you so much. So do not be ungrateful, but always remember to praise God."

The Donkey

In this poem by G.K. Chesterton, the poet describes how ugly the donkey is to most people, both to look at and to listen to. It seems that donkeys have always been despised by people and treated badly. But then the donkey reminds us that it was a donkey who carried Jesus when he rode into Jerusalem and was greeted by a crowd of people. Read the story in *The Bible*, Matthew chapter 21, verses 1-12, before reading the poem.

When fishes flew and forests walked
And figs grew upon thorn.
Some moment when the moon was blood,
Then surely I was born;

With monstrous head and sickening cry
And ears like errant wings,
The devil's walking parody
On all four-footed things.

The tattered outlaw of the earth,
Of ancient crooked will;
Starve, scourge, deride me; I am dumb,
I keep my secret still.

Fools! For I also had my hour;
One far fierce hour and sweet:
There was a shout about my ears,
And palms before my feet!

i   **Animals in Islam**

Although Islam regards humans as being higher than other animals, this does not mean that animals are thought of as simply objects, with no sense or emotions or value to God. The following two passages show how animals are regarded as having both a religious life and a family life.

'All life in the skies and on earth worship Allah, either willingly or in spite of themselves. So too do their shadows bow to Him in the mornings and evenings.'
(Qur'an 13:15)

'There is not an animal that lives on the earth, nor a being that flies on its wings, but forms part of communities like you. Nothing have we omitted from the Book, and they shall all be gathered to their Lord in the end.' (Qur'an 6:38)

Activities

1. a) Look at the passage about St Francis and the birds. Write a prayer that the birds might pray, following St Francis' suggestions about why they should praise God. Then add anything else that you think a bird might want to say to God OR b) Write your own version of a prayer that an animal might pray. Try to make it express what that animal might feel, but also what kind of religious sense you think the animal might have. Look at the information box on Animals in Islam, above, for one view of the religious sense of animals, and at the poem *The Donkey*, for one person's idea about how an animal might feel.

2. Read the story of Balaam and his donkey in the Bible, Numbers 22: 21-34.
a) Why was Balaam angry with his donkey?
b) Why do you think the donkey could see the angel and Balaam could not?
c) Write the story from the donkey's point of view.

3. Some Christian churches regularly hold services for pets and their owners. Do you think the animals themselves benefit from these services? What do they contribute to them?

Playing chicken

Michelle had made the journey many times before. In fact, she thought she knew every bend and turn of the way to her uncle's house. The bus went out of the city and through leafy suburbs. Then it crossed the motorway and started to climb up through countryside and through attractive villages and a small town. Eventually it would turn onto the main road running across the hills and at the village of Crossbend, she would get off. From there it was a two mile walk to her uncle's house. He often picked her up from the bus stop, but this time he wasn't able to. So she had agreed to walk. It was her cousin's birthday and she had been invited to the party. Michelle wasn't that keen on three year olds, but she liked her aunt and uncle.

As she sat on the bus, she found herself thinking about the snatch of discussion she had heard on the radio last night.

"Changing face of the countryside?" she said to herself. "What are they on about? It looks the same as it's always looked. You have fields of crops in some places and fields of animals in other places. Well, there's a field of swedes or something, there's some cabbages and there are animals of some sort over there - are they cows or horses?" As she got nearer she discovered that they were in fact horses belonging to the local riding school and she looked round for some other animals.

She passed a farm entrance that said 'Farm shop - Fresh pork - Home-cured bacon' and she looked in the fields surrounding them for pigs rooting in the hedgerows or rolling in the mud.

There were none. There were large, low, concrete buildings that she supposed must be store-rooms or food preparation rooms. As she travelled on she saw more of them - more than she remembered noticing before. She began to feel as if she was travelling through a strange industrial estate in the heart of the country.

The bus dropped her off and she set off down the road to her uncle's house. He wasn't a farmer. He had been very successful in business and owned his own factory and chain of shops. He had bought an old barn and converted it into a lovely house.

As Michelle walked, she began to peer over hedges to see if she could see any animals. Not much to see was all she found.

Then she came to the sign. It was very bright and new. It said "Country Farm Eggs - as fresh as the dawn". There was a beautiful picture of hens pecking, with a rising sun behind them and a woman in a sunbonnet and an old-fashioned dress proudly watching over them. She knew the farm. Their eggs were in the local supermarket, in boxes with the same picture on them.

"Well," thought Michelle, "there must be some chickens to be seen here." So without much thought, she turned down the little road to take a look. The road was lined with fine trees and swung round sharply to the right, hiding the farmyard from view. Michelle strolled down, enjoying the peace and quiet. Then she came round the corner.

It was not like the picture on the cover of the egg boxes. Here was no romantic farmyard, old farm house or hens scratching. Instead there were three long, low, concrete sheds with corrugated roofs. To one side was a house, which looked like an ordinary town house. As she got closer she could see that downstairs was entirely given over to offices. Parked in the yard were several large vans, each with the idyllic scene of the farmyard painted on the side.

As Michelle hesitated, looking around her, a young man in a business suit came out of the offices.

"Can I help you, young lady? I'm Steve Midhurst." He gave her a broad smile and held out his hand. Automatically Michelle shook hands with him and was a little taken aback at his smart appearance and well-manicured hands - not her idea of a farmer.

Feeling really stupid, Michelle stammered "Actually, I was looking for the chickens. I mean, I was passing, and, well, there don't seem to be any animals about any more, and well, it's sort of ..." Michelle felt herself going redder and redder as she sounded sillier and sillier in her own ears, and Steve grinned at her sympathetically.

"I understand, of course. They're here all right, ninety thousand of them. The thing is, these days we keep chickens nice and warm and dry indoors. There's no wastage from foxes and diseases, their food and water is carefully regulated - no need to scratch around in the dust - and everything they need is right there in front of them. We even give them heat and light so that they can keep laying all year round. It's a much more efficient method of producing eggs. I'd show you the unit, but," (he stood back and looked at her smart clothes) "it's a bit mucky in there. I'm not sure you'd like the smell, either. You off somewhere nice?"

"My uncle's actually - Mr Richards, up at Hillcrest." said Michelle. "Oh, yes, I've heard of Bill Richards. He's done well for himself - a good businessman. I'd like to meet him one day. I tell you what, why don't you jump in my car and I'll run you up there? It's a fair old walk from here." Michelle hesitated. He was very nice but ... no, it wouldn't look right to her uncle.

"No, it's very kind of you, but I'm enjoying the walk, and it's a lovely day, and ... Goodbye, I'd better be off." Michelle retreated as tactfully as she could and set off down the road trying to look as casual and mature as possible.

Later on, after the three year olds had left or gone to sleep, she asked her uncle about the encounter.

"What did he mean, more efficient?" she asked, "Doesn't it make more work to keep the chickens indoors and regulate the warmth and food and everything? It sounds like keeping people in hospital when they could be out looking after themselves and getting their own food."

"The thing is, Michelle, these days in business you have to maximise return on your capital. I mean, in my factory, I can't afford to have machinery lying idle. Once I've paid thousands of pounds for it, it has to keep working day and night. I need to be able to calculate exactly what goes into the production process and what's going to come out. With chickens running round like - well, like chickens! - you can't regulate the output properly. Keep control! that's the secret of productivity. The output from that egg unit has doubled over the last few years, since they've introduced these modern methods. Mrs Wellings who owned it before, was going bust. Now it's an important employer in these parts, and believe me, that's desperately needed."

Different views of animals

Aristotle

Plants exist for the sake of animals, and brute beasts for the sake of man - domestic animals for his use and food, wild ones (or at any rate most of them) for food and other accessories of life, such as clothing and various tools... since nature makes nothing purposeless or in vain, it is undeniably true that she has made animals for the sake of man.
(Aristotle, Politics)

Christian view

Most Christians through the ages have taken the view that animals are to be valued just because God created them. The account in the Bible repeats after each day's creation "and God saw that it was good." But some Christian thinkers at different times have argued that animals and plants were made simply as a mechanism to benefit human beings.

The Battery System of Egg Production

In chapter 8 there is more information about exactly how the chickens are kept under this system. It was introduced after the Second World War to make eggs more readily available to all, and involves keeping

i continued

hens permanently caged in large buildings. In this section we are looking at the way animals can be regarded more as food producing machines than as living beings.

Animals as Machines

In the 17th century, the French philosopher René Déscartes developed the theory that animal bodies are simply machines, although extremely complex machines made by God. Déscartes also described human bodies as machines, with many automatic and programmed responses, but he made a distinction between people and animals by saying that only humans are capable of speech and reason, and only human beings have souls. Some of his followers even went so far as to say that animals had no feelings, and anything that looked like an expression of feeling in an animal was simply an automatic reflex.

Many people, both at the time and later, disagreed with this view, but it has influenced, and continues to influence, the way we treat animals, especially in science and in business. For example, the following passage is quoted from a genetic researcher:

"The cow is an extremely suitable production medium for making these proteins, with no safety or technical problems"
(Otto Postma, quoted in *The Daily Telegraph*, 18.8.89)

Another has written of "...an era of exciting possibilities for rapidly propagating and tailoring animals to meet product and environmental demands"

The following extracts are from an information sheet about egg and chicken production:
"The Chick Hatchery

Inputs: clean hatching eggs from supply farms which have the correct stock, use of correct feed and management techniques...

Outputs: First quality chicks to be delivered to their customers at day-old.

The whole hatchery operation is based on a continuous flow system. At one end, the hatching eggs arrive from the supply farms and they are converted some three weeks later into day-old chicks that come out of the other end.
Production Systems and Bird Welfare

Today's hybrid hen has been bred for efficient egg production and is capable of laying on average 280 eggs during a twelve months laying period. Hens are normally kept in production for a period of 12 to 18 months before being replaced by point-of-lay pullets at 18 weeks of age.
(From notes to National Farmers Union video, *The Chicken and the Egg*)"

Activities

1. In the story, how do you think Steve Midhurst feels about the laying hens? Complete the following sentence as if you were Steve. You can use one or more of the words below, or think of your own.

"I am in charge of ninety thousand laying hens. They are..."

[profitable; happy; comfortable; smelly; efficiently managed; working hard for me; imprisoned; hidden away; well-treated; our fellow-creatures; dumb animals; God's creatures]

What do you think Michelle's uncle would say? "Steve is in charge of..." etc. Use the same list of words, or your own.

What would Michelle say?

Remember that both Michelle and her uncle are Christians. Do you think this will make a difference to what they say?

2. How you write about an animal or a machine depends on how you feel about it, or how you want other people to feel about it. Look in books, magazines, TV advertisements and try to find examples of:

a) animals described as if they were objects, e.g. 'the product'. Look in, for example, encyclopedia articles or books on stock-breeding, reports of scientific experiments.

b) objects described or presented as if they were animals or people. This is especially common in TV ads - cars choosing their own oil, toilets being happy because the germs have been killed, a helpful talking stairlift, for example.

3. Making animals seem like objects, or objects seem like animals or people, is usually done to encourage a certain way of treating them. Think of something that you believe is OK to do to an object but not OK to do to, for example, a dog or some other animal (including perhaps human beings). Make a poster, or a short dramatic scene like a TV advert, trying to persuade people either that it is wrong to do this to a particular object, or that it is OK to do it to the animal you have chosen. (For example, if you believe that it is wrong to kick the cat to express your bad temper, but OK to kick the wall, try to persuade people that it is cruel to kick walls, no matter how you feel!)

4. Much science-fiction (both books and films) has been written around the idea that machines or robots could be created with human or animal characteristics (K9 in 'Star Wars', Number Five in 'Short Circuit', Kryten in 'Red Dwarf'). Imagine you are setting out to design robots to replace the following animals. First of all you will need to decide what good the animals themselves are. Then write down what characteristics each robot would have to have to make a satisfactory substitute. If there are functions you think the robot could not perform, write them down at the end of your list.

a) a household animal such as a dog or cat

b) a farm animal such as a sheep or a horse

c) a wild animal such as a badger or a whale.

You will need to think carefully why people want such animals in the world. Is it because they are decorative, they make the world a more interesting place, they provide a sense of adventure, or what?

5. Find out about how animals are regarded in different religions. Use the information on pages 22, 24, 39-41, and the passages on pages 18, 19 and 20. Choose one religion and make a poster or a leaflet from the point of view of that religion, arguing against the idea that we can use animals in any way we like because they are there for our use.

A Buddhist Jataka Story

Buddhists follow the teachings of Siddharta Gautama, who became the Buddha when he found truth and enlightenment. But they teach that this great truth was not found all in one lifetime. In previous lives, whether human or animal, the future Buddha had lived a good and wise life, often giving his own life for the sake of others and loving and helping all whom he met. These stories are called Jataka tales, and this is one about his life as a dog. It raises some questions about how people think of animals, and how they treat animals because of this.

There was once a king who had a beautiful chariot, drawn by six white horses, with beautiful leather harnesses. One day the chariot and harness was accidentally left out in the rain overnight in the palace courtyard, and the beautiful leather became wet and soft. The dogs who lived in the palace saw this and seized their chance to have some fun. All night they chewed and gnawed at the straps, and by morning, when the dogs quietly slipped away, the whole harness was ruined.

The king was furious when he found out. It was clear that this was the work of dogs, so the king ordered all the dogs in the city to be killed. There were hundreds of dogs in the city and they were distressed when they heard the news. They went together to tell the one who was their leader, for he loved and protected them. The chief dog thought about it and realised that it could only have been the palace dogs who were to blame - no other dogs could get into the courtyard.

So in spite of the danger, he set off alone to see the king. On every street corner there were men ready to kill any dog they saw, as the king had ordered, but when they saw this dog, with eyes so full of love, they did not touch him. When he came to the palace, the guards on the gate were so struck by his appearance that they let him through into the king's presence. The courtiers stood around, but silence fell as they all gazed at his eyes, full of sorrow and love. At long last the dog spoke.

"Great king, is it your command that all dogs of the city should be killed?"

"Yes", replied the king, "It is my command."

"What harm have they done?" the dog asked.

"They have destroyed my leather harness", replied the king.

"Which dogs did this?"

"I do not know. That is why I have ordered all dogs to be killed."

"Is every dog to be killed? Or are some dogs going to live?" enquired the chief dog.

"Only the royal dogs in the place will be spared", said the king.

In a gentle voice the dog enquired, "O king, is this just? Why have you decided that the dogs in the city must be guilty and the dogs in the palace innocent? Isn't it simply because you are friendly with the dogs in the palace, but you never see the dogs in the city?"

The king thought for a while, then said,

"Wise chief, tell me then, who are the guilty ones?"

"Undoubtedly it is the royal dogs," replied the dog.

"Can you prove this to me?" demanded the king.

"Order that the royal dogs be brought here and given kusa grass and buttermilk to eat," said the chief dog.

So they were brought and given kusa grass and buttermilk and before long, shreds of leather came out of their mouths and fell on the ground. The guilty ones were found.

The king rose from his throne. "Your words are true and wise and I shall never forget you as long as you live. I shall give orders that the dogs of the city be given care and food every day of their lives."

That wise and brave dog was, of course, the future Buddha.

Activities

1. a) In the story, how did the king regard the palace dogs and the town dogs? Write one sentence that he might have said about each.
b) Why did the king assume that the town dogs were to blame?
c) At the end of the story, what actions do you think the king should take?

2. Like the king in the story, people often care more about the animals they see every day and are familiar with, than they do about animals they never see. Conduct a survey amongst people who are not studying this book to see how common this attitude is:

a) Give a number of people copies of the two survey forms on page 93. If you wish, add a few more animals to the list before you copy it. Try to ask a wide variety of ages, occupations, different families, etc.
b) For each sheet, add up the total scores given to the different animals by everyone in your survey. You should end up with a total popularity score and a total frequency score for each animal.
c) Make a histogram showing the popularity and the frequency score side by side for each animal.

The frequency score is always likely to be higher than the popularity score, but does a particularly high frequency score go with a high popularity score?

Discuss in class what you think your results might mean.

3. There are many stories about talking animals. Some well-known examples are the Dr Dolittle stories of Hugh Loftus, the Narnia books by C.S. Lewis.

Read one of these and discuss what difference it makes to our attitude that people can talk to these animals. Are they seen simply as people? Do they still have animal characteristics? How would the people in the story treat them? See especially the scene in *The Silver Chair* where Puddleglum and the children discover they are eating talking deer, not just any deer. Why are they so shocked?

CHAPTER 4

Rights and Duties

We hear a great deal about human rights, animal rights, someone having a right to do something or other. Where do these rights come from? Who decides what is a universal right and what happens if not everyone agrees? Who qualifies as having rights in relation to someone else? Throughout the history of Europe, there seems to have been a tendency for rights that were originally only granted to a few, to be extended further and further, first to a wider group of people, and more recently to animals and to the earth as a whole.

It shouldn't happen to ...

Joseph had never seen Leila look so angry.

"How could you?" she hissed at Michelle, "You knew how important it was to me. You had no right to let me down like that!"

"Oh, come on," said Michelle, looking a little bit shame-faced, "I said I'm sorry, didn't I? I changed my mind, that's all. It's no big deal."

"No, not to you - of course not to you. It's all you, you, you, isn't it?", and Leila pointedly turned her back on Michelle as the lesson started.

At break, Joseph found the others and asked them, "What's going on? It's not like Leila to get in such a state."

"No, but she's got a right to be angry," said Christine. "She and Michelle had arranged to go into town on Saturday, look round the shops and see that new film that's on. Michelle rang up at the last minute and cancelled. Leila's parents won't let her go into town on her own, so that meant she couldn't go at all."

"Well, it's a shame for Leila, but these things happen," said Joseph, "I suppose something came up and she couldn't go."

"That's what Leila thought, and she wasn't going to make a fuss until she got into school this morning and discovered that the only reason Michelle cancelled was that she discovered there was something on telly she didn't want to miss. She'd just not considered Leila's feelings at all. None of us have the right to treat people like that."

"Oh, come on Christine," said Joseph, "I think you and Leila are making too much of this. OK, she's upset, she was disappointed, but that's life. Things happen that we don't like. If we all went round blaming other people and talking about rights, it'll begin to sound like that case in the paper the other day. Did you see it? Apparently a young woman in the States was due to go out with some guy, so she went out and bought a new dress and bag and so on. Anyway, she spent about seventy dollars. Then the guy stands her up. Just doesn't turn up. There she is standing by the town hall clock or something, and he doesn't show. So what does she do? She sues him. Takes him to court because he denied her right to be happy. She tried to sue him for the seventy dollars she had spent and another hundred dollars for 'suffering'. Talk about daft! But you and Leila are heading in that direction, with your 'had no right' all the time. If it comes to rights, Michelle had the right to change her mind, didn't she?"

"I can see why you're worried, Joseph," said Gavin, "I mean, if that idea spread to Britain, then any girls going out with you could claim thousands of pounds in psychological damage and denial of happiness cases!"

"No, come on, Gavin," said Pallavi, "It's not funny, Leila's really upset. She would never do anything like that to anyone and she doesn't deserve to have it done to her. She's given up things sometimes when Michelle wanted her to and she ought to be able to expect the same in return."

"No Pallavi, you're missing the point!" said Christine, "People don't have to deserve their rights. Leila's a person, her feelings are just as important as Michelle's. She's got a right to expect basic human decency from everyone, whether she's done anything for them before or not."

"What do you mean Christine?" asked Pallavi, "Are you saying that it doesn't matter what people have done, doesn't matter who they are or how they treat others, they've still got rights? Surely we have to earn the right to be treated well, by treating others as we would want to be treated?"

"No, I'm not sure that we do. We may have to fight for our rights, like the suffragettes and others had to fight for the vote or for equal pay for women. And I'm glad they did fight, so that I can have those things. But they were claiming what was theirs, not earning a favour. I don't have to do anything to earn those, they're mine by right. If you start saying anything else, it's too easy to take away people's rights."

"That's all very well," interrupted Joseph, "But who says you've got those rights? It's only governments who can give rights and we've seen often enough in history that they can take them away again just as quick. No one has a God-given right to say 'Give me the vote,' or 'Give me a job'. If the government won't or can't give it to you, you've got no rights. That's just tough. It's the way the world is."

"No, that can't be right," said Gavin, suddenly serious. "There are right and wrong ways of behaving. People ought to be able to expect proper treatment. I don't know, perhaps some rights are 'God-given', as you say. There are stories in The Bible where God gets angry about injustice."

"Why, why, why," sighed Christine, "do you have to bring God into it every time? Isn't it time that people grew up and started taking on their own responsibility? People's rights are something logical and natural, nothing to do with God. When people talk about 'God-given rights', they're usually handing out injustice, not justice. We can do better than that."

"Oh, typical," said Joseph, "I used to say that you thought you were God. Now it turns out you're actually better than God."

"I didn't say that! I . . . ."

Christine was interrupted by the urgent ringing of the fire-bell.

"Oh no!" wailed Pallavi, "we don't have to go out, do we? It's cold and wet. They can't make us!"

"Hm," said Gavin, "I wonder. Can they make us? Do they have the right? If there really is a fire, would I be violating Christine's right of free speech if I tell her to shut up lecturing and get out of here? If Pallavi's hair gets wet and she catches a cold, can she sue the school? Should Joseph be threatening me like that?..."

Gavin was still jabbering away as Joseph dragged him out into the carpark, and the four of them caught sight of Michelle making her way towards Leila, who was standing alone in the rain.

---

i   Declarations of Rights

At different periods in history, in different places, many thinkers and politicians have drawn up systematic lists of rights. They vary greatly, both in terms of what rights are laid down and in terms of who is regarded as having rights. They also vary in terms of their arguments about where these rights come from. Some speak in religious terms, for example "God created humans more intelligent than other animals, so that gives them the right to decide how animals would live." Others speak in terms of the logic by which society can work, for example, "If people did not have the right to keep what they work for, then no one would do any work."

'The Magna Carta', signed by King John in 1215, protects the rights of the barons, the church, and 'free men'.

In 1789 the French National Assembly accepted a 'Declaration of the Rights of man and the Citizen'. These were:

representation in the law-making process
equality before the law
equality of opportunity
freedom from imprisonment without good reason
freedom of speech and religion
taxation in proportion to ability to pay
security of property.

The following rights were added to this in 1946:
equal rights for women
right to work, join a union and strike
leisure, social security and support in old age
free education

The American Declaration of Independence, 1776, was based on what were seen as the basic rights of everyone to 'life, liberty and the pursuit of happiness' - but black slavery was still legal.

In 1948 the United Nations drew up the Universal Declaration of Human Rights which stated:
1. All human beings are born free and

i continued

equal in dignity and rights...
3. Everyone has the right to life, liberty and security of person.
4. No one shall be held in slavery or servitude; slavery and the slave trade shall be prohibited in all their forms.
5. No one shall be subjected to torture or to cruel, inhuman or degrading treatment or punishment.

   The extension of the idea of rights to all races, both sexes, to children, animals and the rest of the natural world, has been a gradual process, not accepted by everyone.

Rights and duties
The idea of people, animals, or even the earth, having rights is a common one in our society but many faiths do not talk about rights. Their teaching turns the idea round and lays down what each person's duty is towards each other, towards God and towards all of his creation.

Activities

1. In groups, make a story or a play based on one of the following phrases:
'You have no right...'
'We demand the right...'
'I have the right...'

2. In the story, different people express different opinions about rights. What is your opinion about the following statements?
'None of us have the right to be inconsiderate to others.'
'Everyone has the right to be happy.'
'You have to earn your rights by behaving well yourself'
'Some rights are given by God'

3. Find information about one particular declaration of rights, for example the French 'Declaration of the Rights of Man', or the USA's Bill of Rights. Write down:
 a. Who is regarded as having rights? (For example, all citizens, all adults, all males.)
b. Can you think of a group that is not protected by these rights that you think ought to be included?
 c. What is seen as the basis of these rights? (For example, are they laid down by God, are they seen as natural and logical, are they based on what works in practice?)
 d. What particular rights are regarded as universal?

4. In groups, draw up your own 'bill of rights', based on the ideas discussed in question 3.
5. In all these different declarations of rights, who is responsible for making sure that they are kept? What does each individual have to do?

6. When people are describing a particularly evil act, they often use words such as 'the people who did this are not human beings, they are... ('devils', or 'animals', or some other non-human description). When they describe someone whose brain activity and abilities are severely limited, they may say that they are a 'vegetable'. Do you think there is a certain level of behaviour and/or ability which is necessary to qualify someone as a human being and as having rights?

The Donkey's Messenger

On a lonely mountain road in Ethiopia, two travellers met. They both had donkeys heavily laden with goods, struggling up the steep road. The two travellers stopped to exchange greetings and news and sat down by the side of the road to chat. The two donkeys also stopped and moved slowly towards each other. One of them pushed its head forward curiously. At once the owner of the other donkey jumped up, shouting, and hit the donkey on the nose.

"Get off, you brute, get off!"

"Stop, stop!" cried the other man, "Why did you do that?"

"Didn't you see?" shouted the first man. "He was reaching forward to take some of the grain out of my donkey's sack! Greedy beast!"

"No, no" came the reply, "He wasn't after food. Don't you know that all donkeys reach their heads forward to each other when they meet?"

"No, I didn't know that. What on earth for?"

"Well, you know how donkeys have been treated by humans since time immemorial. They carry heavy loads, they are beaten, they get the poorest food to eat, and they are called stupid and obstinate. Well, donkeys don't like that any more than you or I would. They got together many, many years ago, and they chose one of their number to be their messenger to heaven to ask for help. And meanwhile, the other donkeys have gone on patiently enduring the treatment we give them. But every time one donkey meets another, he stretches out his head in the hope that it is the messenger returned from heaven with news that help is on the way."

St Werburgh and the Geese

St Werburgh was Abbess of Wedon in Northamptonshire in the 7th century. One day the tenants who lived on the abbey land came to her and complained that the village geese, which roamed freely, were destroying their crops, and if this continued, everyone would go hungry in the winter.

St Werburgh sent for all the geese and put them in a pen. The next day she went to the pen and found the geese in great distress.

"Oh Abbess, give us back our freedom," they pleaded. "We will not eat the crops any more, but only the grass that grows in the meadows and the grubs and worms that we can find."

"Is that a promise?" asked St Werburgh, and when the geese assured her that they would keep their side of the bargain if she would only let them go, she gave orders to the abbey servants to let the geese wander freely again.

"Don't worry, they will not eat your crops," she told the villagers.
But the next day the geese came back to the abbey, still in great distress.

"You promised that we would all be released," they said, "but when we got back to our meadows we discovered that one goose was missing. We cannot keep our promise if you do not keep yours".

St Werburgh made inquiries and discovered that one of the abbey servants had kept a goose back and killed it for food.

"Bring me the body of the goose!" commanded Werburgh.

"I am afraid I cannot," said the servant, "My family have already eaten it, and all we have left are the bones."

"Then bring me those," ordered St Werburgh.

When the bones were brought to her, she miraculously restored the flesh, the feathers and the life of the bird and it happily rejoined the flock.

"We made an agreement with the geese," said St Werburgh. "We cannot expect them to keep their side of the bargain if we do not keep ours."

The Camel

From the Hadith (accounts of Muhammad's life and sayings)
After the Muslims had established themselves at Medina, they planted gardens and trees. One day the Prophet Muhammad was walking through Medina and came to a particularly pleasant garden. One man was sitting in the shade of a tree and others were sitting in cool parts of the garden. In one corner was a camel tied to a post and howling. Muhammad went over to it and saw that it was in great distress. Not only was it tied up in the full heat of the sun, it was thin and exhausted and in poor condition.

Muhammad stroked and soothed the camel for a while, until it became calmer. Then he turned to the people in the garden.

"Whose camel is this?" he asked

"It's mine" said the man in the shade of the tree.

"Aren't you ashamed of yourself?" asked the Prophet, "Allah has entrusted this creature to you, for it to help you by working for you, but also for you to care for it. This is one of God's living creatures and you are responsible for its well-being. How dare you sit at your ease in the shade, when the creature entrusted to your care is suffering!"

i   Why be kind to animals?

Although all faiths have teachings about the way animals ought to be treated, they have very different views about why they should be treated in a certain way.

Judaism:

Animals are to be cared for and respected because they are God's creation. The fifth of the Ten Commandments lays down that all should rest on the Sabbath Day including animals: "On it you shall not do any work, neither you, nor your son or daughter, nor your manservant or maidservant, nor your ox, your donkey, or any of your animals..." (Deuteronomy 5:14). This has been described as 'the first animal right in history'.

Once when the Master, the holy Ari, was sitting in the House of Study with his disciples, he looked at one of them and said to him: "Go out from here, for today you are excommunicated from heaven." The disciple fell at the feet of the Master and said to him: "What is my sin? I will repent for it."

So the Master said to him: "It is because of the chickens you have at home. You have not fed them for two days and they cry out to God in their hunger. God will forgive you on condition you see to it that before you leave for prayers in the morning you give food to your chickens. For they are dumb animals and they cannot ask for their food."
(The Wisdom of the Jewish Mystics, Alan Unterman, Sheldon Press 1976, quoted in Faith and Nature, Palmer, Nash and Hattingh, WWF 1987)

There was once a Jewish Rabbi who was accustomed to attending country fairs, and there to do good offices to those in need. Once it befell that some cattle breeders had left their animals standing in the market place with their thirst unslaked, while their owners attended to their affairs elsewhere. The Rabbi, perceiving this, made the rounds with a bucket and gave the calves their drink. A dealer, returning from an errand and seeing a stranger thus employed, mistook him for a hired man, and commanded him to give drink to his cattle. The Rabbi obeyed, and after having performed his chore, was offered a coin. He laughingly refused, saying, "Get thee hence, man; I did not do thy bidding, but God's, Who commands us to be merciful to His creatures."
(Adapted from The Hasidic Anthology, selected by Louis I. Newman, Blech Publishing Company, New York, 1944. Quoted in Faith and Nature)

Islam:

Doing good to beast is like the doing of good to human beings, a deed of charity; while cruelty to animals is forbidden (Mishkat al Masabih, vol.2)

All creatures are God's dependants and the most beloved to God, among them, is he who does good to God's dependants. (Kashf al-Khafa')

There is a story about a Prophet who wanted to destroy a whole ants' nest because one of the ants had bitten him. God reproached him, saying, "Have you destroyed a whole community that glorifies Me because of one ant that bit you?"
(Muslim, quoted in Islam and Ecology, Khalid and O'Brien, Cassell 1992)

i continued

Hinduism:

"One should treat animals such as deer, camels, asses, monkeys, mice, snakes, birds and flies exactly as one's own son. How little difference there actually is between children and these innocent animals."

(Srimad Bhagavatam 7:14:9. Quoted in *Seeds of Truth* by Ranchor Prime)

Jains:

"One who neglects or disregards the existence of earth, air, fire, water and vegetation disregards his own existence which is entwined with them."

"You are that which you intend to harm."

(Mahavira, quoted in the Jain *Declaration on Nature*)

Buddhism:

Whatever living beings there may be;
Whether they are weak or strong, omitting none,
The great or the mighty, medium, short or small,
The seen and the unseen,
Those living near and far away,
Those born and to-be-born -
May all beings be at ease!
Let none deceive another,
Or despise any being in any state.
Let none through anger or ill-will
Wish harm upon another.
Even as a mother protects with her life
Her child, her only child,
So with a boundless heart
should one cherish all living beings.

(Metta Sutta)

Reincarnation

Hindus believe that every living creature, human or animal, embodies a spark of the universal atman, or spirit. Each individual is reborn many times into a different body. Everything that you do, say or think determines what will happen to you in the future, whether in this life or a later life. This is the law of karma. It is not a question of reward and punishment, but rather cause and effect. You are reborn in a body which suits the thoughts, actions and desires of your previous life. If, in each life, you try to live in as good a way as possible, you will progress to a higher body. Eventually, when you have lived many thousands of lives and become more spiritually developed, you may be free from the cycle of birth and death.

Humans are thought of as being higher than most animals in this sense, because they are more aware of spiritual things, they have the ability to think about good and bad. Other animals which are thought to be high up on the path to freedom are snakes, monkeys and especially cows.

Sikhs and Buddhists also believe in reincarnation.

Only one life

Christians, Jews and Muslims believe that each person has only one life and must live that life in the best way they can, because they will not have another chance. They also believe that there is a life after death which depends on how people have lived their life on earth. Most Humanists, too, believe that everyone has only one life, but that death is the end - there is nothing beyond it and people only live on in the memory of

i continued

those who knew them or the results of their actions.

Judgement

Many Christians, Jews and Muslims say that everyone will be judged on what they have done in this life. But it is also important that this is not what should concern people most. People should be aiming to please God in their lives because of love, not because of fear.

Most Christians, Jews and Muslims believe that God will judge everyone in the world and give rewards or punishments according to how they have lived their life. Some believe that this will take place as soon as the person dies, others believe that there will be a Day of Judgement at the end of time. Beliefs differ about how God will judge people: whether it is on their belief, their actions or both.

Rights of animals in Islam

Although Islamic teaching puts emphasis on each person's duty towards others, the system of Muslim law lays down rights as well, and animals are included in those who have rights. The traditions about the sayings and deeds of the Prophet Muhammad have several references to the treatment of animals. Animals do not have the same rights as people, for example domestic animals are the property of their owner and can be bought and sold, but they must be treated with respect and without cruelty. Wild animals can be hunted for food or skins, but not to put them in cages or to use them as entertainment. Animals that are harming humans can be killed if necessary, but not indiscriminately. In the thirteenth century a Muslim scholar, working from the stories and sayings of

the Prophet, made the following statement of human duties towards domestic animals and those that are hunted:

i   Give them the provision that their species requires, even if they are old and sick so that they are of no benefit to you;

ii   Do not burden them beyond what they can bear;

iii   Do not put them together with anything that might injure them, either other animals or objects;

iv   Slaughter them with kindness and do not cut up their bodies until they are cold and completely lifeless;

v   Do not slaughter their young where they can see it;

vi   Give them comfortable resting and feeding places;

vii   Put males and females together during their mating seasons;

viii   If you hunt game, only kill what you can use, and do not use a weapon that breaks their bones, but one that kills quickly and cleanly.

The Five Freedoms

The Farm Animal Welfare Council was established in 1979 to advise the UK Government on the welfare of animals on farms, when being transported, and at the place of slaughter. They have formulated a list of 'Five Freedoms' which can act as a guide for animal welfare. They do not put these forward as 'rights' that animals have, but as a description of an ideal state by which to measure what actually happens:

i   Freedom from hunger and thirst, by ready access to fresh water and a diet to maintain full health and vigour.

i **continued**

disease, by prevention or rapid diagnosis and treatment.

ii Freedom from discomfort, by providing an appropriate environment including shelter and a comfortable resting area.

iii Freedom from pain, injury or

iv Freedom to express normal behaviour, by providing sufficient space, proper facilities and company of the animal's own kind.

v Freedom from fear and distress, by

Activities

1. What do you think each of the stories on pages 35–36 is saying about the rights of animals? Notice that all three of the stories are about animals that are used to serve humans.

2. Do you think that animals ought to be included in a declaration of rights? Do you think that their rights should be the same as those of human beings? Do rights depend on which animals we are talking about? Make a list of different animals, insects, fish etc. and discuss whether what you have said above applies to each of them.

3. In groups, draw up a declaration of animal rights, including any limitation of rights you think ought to be there. (For example, you may wish to consider that no animal right should interfere with a fundamental human right.)

4. Make a poster or leaflet to publicise and argue in favour of the animal rights you have drawn up in question 3. Compare the arguments used in each person's poster or leaflet. As a class, try to group the arguments into types. For example, are there some based on asking 'how would you like it?', some based on religious belief and some based on an idea of universal human rights etc.

5. Look at the information box about rights and duties in Islam. Take your list of rights of animals, and turn it round into a list of duties of human beings. Be as specific as you can. Are there some things that you have listed as rights that cannot be changed into duties? Do you think humans have some duties towards animals that cannot be expressed as animal rights?

Rights and Wants, Need and Greed

What happens if one group's rights and wants conflict with another's?

Lalo and Malik

A Sikh story tells of the time that Guru Nanak stayed in a certain village with a poor carpenter called Lalo. A rich man called Malik was offended that the Guru had decided to stay with the humble carpenter rather than with him. He invited Guru Nanak to a meal at his house. The Guru came, but did not eat any of the rich food that was put before him. Angrily, Malik asked him,

'Why do you eat the hard bread that Lalo gives you, but you won't eat the delicious food that I am offering?'

'I will show you,' said Guru Nanak. He asked someone to fetch a piece of bread from Lalo's house, and taking hold of it, he squeezed it. Milk came out of the bread. Then he picked up some of the food from Malik's table, and squeezed it. To everyone's horror, blood came out of it.

'Your food has been gained from the hardship of others' said Guru Nanak, 'Lalo's food has been gained by his own hard toil.'

---

i   Religious teachings on need and greed

From the Hindu Scriptures

"Everything in the Universe belongs to the Lord. You should therefore only take what is really necessary for yourself, which is set aside for you. You should not take anything else, because you know to whom it belongs"
(Isa Upanishad, verse 1, quoted in Seeds of Truth by Ranchor Prime)

From constant thinking about objects of the senses attachment arises. From that attachment, desire develops, and from desire, anger arises. From anger, delusion arises. From delusion comes confusion of memory. From confusion of memory come loss of discrimination. When discrimination is lost, you fall down into the material pool again.
Bhagavad Gita 2.62-63 (Essential teachings of Hinduism p.56)

Buddhism:

And how is a monk contented? Here, a monk is satisfied with a robe to protect his body, with alms to satisfy his stomach, and having accepted sufficient, he goes on his way. Just as a bird with wings flies hither and thither, burdened by nothing but its wings, so is he satisfied. In this way, Sire, a monk is contented.
Digh Nikaya, Vol.1, page 71. (Quoted in Essential Teachings of Buddhism, p. 23)

Buddhism teaches that a monk only has four basic needs:
food which is given freely;
a set of three robes;
shelter for one night;
medicine for illness.

Christianity

Therefore I tell you, do not worry about your life, what you will eat or drink; or about your body, what you will wear. Is not life more important than food, and the body more important than clothes? Look at the birds of the air; they do not sow or reap or store away in barns, and yet your heavenly father feeds them. Are you not much more valuable than they?
Matthew 6:25-26

Judaism

Woe to you who add house to house and join field to field till no space is left and you live alone in the land.
Isaiah 5:8

Islam

Those who, when they spend, are not

---

i continued

extravagant and not niggardly but hold a just balance between those extremes,... Those are the ones who will be rewarded with the highest place in heaven.
(Qur'an 225, 67 and 75)

The Prophet Muhammad is reported to have said -
Two hungry wolves if let loose among a flock of sheep, will not do more damage than that which is caused by a man's avarice for wealth and status in preference to his religion.
(As recorded by Tirmizi)

All forms of wasteful behaviour are forbidden in Islam. Over-indulgence, excesses and unnecessary luxuries are to be avoided.

Social utilities in Islam may be divided into three levels: necessities, conveniences and refinements. Necessities are all activities and things that are essential for a good individual and social life; conveniences are things that are not vital but may be needed to make life much easier; refinements include activities and things that go beyond convenience and may be said to be luxuries

Activities

1. Read the story of Lalo and Malik. Do you think that Malik had a right to the food that he was offering Guru Nanak? Give reasons for your answer.

2. Guru Nanak said that people had suffered to provide the food that Malik was offering. Take one food that you might offer to a guest or eat on a special occasion and find out as much as you can about the way it is produced. In particular, find out whether any people or animals suffer in the process.

3. Look at the information about Buddhism and the needs of a monk. What are the differences between this and the list on page 43 of the basic needs of animals? Why do you think the lists are different?

4. In a light-hearted way, think of a food or drink that you should have more of. This can be for any reason, for example, you really like it, or you believe it is good for you. Make a political-style speech to the rest of the class, arguing why your chosen food should be more freely available to all and what steps you think should be taken to bring this about. Be as persuasive as you can, even if you don't seriously believe that this should happen!

5. *We have written the following exercise in relation to eggs. If you prefer, or if you do not eat eggs at all for any reason, do the following exercise in relation to a different food, for example sugar, milk, or fruit. When you have done it, compare your answers with those of someone who does eat eggs.*

A recent video about egg production states that forty years ago there were 'insufficient eggs' produced in this country.

a) Make a list of the foods you ate this week which contained eggs. Estimate how many eggs this adds up to. (This may be difficult if you had, for example, a slice of cake, but try to make an educated guess.)

b) On your list, give each item a mark based on how important you believe it was for you to eat that item:

> 0 means you think it was simply being greedy and you would have been better off without it.
>
> 1 means you think it was purely for enjoyment, but did no harm.
>
> 2 means you think it was the tastiest way of meeting your nutritional needs at the time.
>
> 3 means you think it was essential for your nutritional needs at the time.

c) How many fewer eggs would you have eaten if you had cut out all the 0's and 1's?

d) What substitutes could you find for the 2's and 3's?

e) On the basis of your marking, how many eggs would you say you 'needed'?

f) If there were a shortage of eggs, what would be the best thing to do about it?

6. With changing tastes and changing availability, ideas of 'treats', or 'luxury foods' change over time. For example, the apprentices of London once demanded that they should not be given salmon to eat more than once a week.

a) Write down what foods you or your family have when you want a treat, or a celebration meal.

b) What makes these foods special? For example, are they expensive, difficult or time-consuming to prepare, hard to buy, or perhaps only available in season? Or is it simply that your family do not normally eat them?

c) Compare the lists of everyone in the class and make a graph of the most common food treats.

d) Repeat steps a) to c), but this time asking older people, such as parents or grandparents, what were the food treats they looked forward to as children.

e) Compare the two graphs. What has changed? Can you find reasons for the changes?

CHAPTER 5

Do all Animals Deserve the Same?

Our reaction to different animals varies from person to person and from culture to culture. Some people are afraid of snakes, others are fascinated by them. Can we say that some animals matter more than others? If we kill a fly or a slug, is it different from killing a cat or a dog? This section explores the differences we make between different animal species.

The following two poems express very different feelings about bats. You do not need to understand the whole poem, but read each one to get an idea of how the poet is thinking about the bats.

Bat by D.H. Lawrence

At evening, sitting on this terrace,
When the sun from the west, beyond Pisa, beyond the mountains of Carrara
Departs, and the world is taken by surprise...
When the tired flower of Florence is in gloom beneath the glowing
Brown hills surrounding...
When under the arches of the Ponte Vecchio
A green light enters against stream, flush from the west,
Against the current of obscure Arno...
Look up, and you see things flying
Between the day and the night;
Swallows with spools of dark thread sewing the shadows together.
A circle swoop, and a quick parabola under the bridge arches
Where light pushes through;
A sudden turning upon itself of a thing in the air
A dip to the water.
And you think:
'The swallows are flying so late!'
Swallows?
Dark air-life looping
Yet missing the pure loop...
A twitch, a twitter, an elastic shudder in flight
And serrated wings under the sky,
Like a glove, a black glove thrown up at the light,

And falling back.
Never swallows!
Bats!
The swallows are gone.
At a wavering instant the swallows gave way to bats
By the Ponte Vecchio...
Changing guard.
Bats, and an uneasy creeping in one's scalp
As the bats swoop overhead!
Flying madly.
Pipistrello!
Black piper on an infinitesimal pipe.
Little lumps that fly in the air and have voices indefinite, wildly vindictive;
Wings like bits of umbrella
Bats!
Creatures that hang themselves up like an old rag, to sleep;
And disgustingly upside down.
Hanging upside down like rows of disgusting old rags
And grinning in their sleep.
Bats!
In China the bat is symbol of happiness
Not for me!

Bats by Randall Jarrell

A bat is born
Naked and blind and pale.
His mother makes a pocket of her tail
And catches him. He clings to her long fur
By his thumbs and toes and teeth.
And then the mother dances through the night
Doubling and looping, soaring, somersaulting -
Her baby hangs on underneath.
All night, in happiness, she hunts and flies.
Her high sharp cries
Like shining needlepoints of sound
Go out into the night and, echoing back,
Tell her what they have touched.
She hears how far it is, how big it is,
Which way it's going:
She lives by hearing.
The mother eats the moths and gnats she catches
In full flight; in full flight
The mother drinks the water of the pond
She skims across. Her baby hangs on tight.
Her baby drinks the milk she makes him
In moonlight or starlight, in mid-air.

Their single shadow, printed on the moon
Or fluttering across the stars,
Whirls on all night; at daybreak
The tired mother flaps home to her rafter.
The others are all there.
They hang themselves up by their toes,
They wrap themselves in their brown wings.
Bunched upside-down, they sleep in air.
Their sharp ears, their sharp teeth, their quick sharp faces
Are dull and slow and mild.
All the bright day, as the mother sleeps,
She folds her wings about her sleeping child.

Activities

1. Look at the last two lines of the poem by D. H. Lawrence. Does it seem odd to you that the bat should be a symbol of happiness? What feelings do you have about bats? Make a collection as a class about the images of bats that are commonly used.

2. How did Lawrence describe the flying creatures when he thought they were swallows? How did he feel about them when he discovered that they were bats? Pick out some of the phrases he uses to describe the bats which show how he feels about them.

3. How does Randall Jarrell feel about the bats? Pick out some of the phrases he uses to describe them which show how he feels.

4. Compare the way the two poems describe the bats sleeping. Why are they different? Is one of them true and the other not true?

5. Animals are often spoken or written about in ways that say a great deal about the attitude of the person describing them.

a) Guess what animals are being described here, then discuss your answers with each other:
a four-legged friend
an animal with dirty habits
an animal that works hard
a slimy animal
an animal with a good memory
a faithful animal
aggressive animals that came from the jungles of Asia. (This expression is quoted from a video about chickens!)
b) How did each description make you feel about the animal?
c) Make your own list of descriptions of animals. Try to make the description match how you feel about the animal, or how other people might feel about it. Try out your descriptions on a partner.

6. Animals are also used in advertisements or films to create an atmosphere or a feeling. For example, an advertisement about car crime shows jackals, an advertisement for petrol shows a tiger.
a) Make a collection list of further examples.
b) What feelings or attitudes are aroused by this way of describing things?
c) Why have the writers or film-makers chosen this way of expressing it?

6. You may have read *The Sheep-Pig* by Dick King-Smith or Charlotte's Web by E. B. White (Puffin). Although they are written mainly for younger readers many older people enjoy reading them.

In *The Sheep Pig* , a pig learns to herd sheep. Falsely accused of the slaughter of the ewe who is his friend, he is narrowly saved from becoming bacon, and goes on to be champion at the sheep-dog trials. In Charlotte's Web , Wilbur, the runt pig is saved from the slaughter house by the wit of his spider friend, Charlotte, but then Charlotte herself dies.

Both books make the reader think about our assumptions about different species of animals. If you have read either of the books:

a) Did you feel differently about either pigs or spiders after you had read the book? Find a passage in one of the books that shows how one of the characters changed their mind about another animal.
b) In what ways does the author describe the animals so as to make people think differently about them? Find a paragraph in one of the books that shows this.

7. a) Take an animal that you are fond of or find attractive, e.g. dog, cat, lamb, robin, and write about it to make it sound as unpleasant as possible. Think about:
a related animal that is less attractive, for example you might describe a dog as a 'savage wolf';
an aspect of its appearance that can be compared to something unattractive;
an aspect of its way of life that is unattractive (you may need to do some research on your chosen animal to find this).

b) Do the same in reverse: take an animal that you dislike or fear and describe it in a way that makes it attractive. This will probably be harder. If you have read *Charlotte's Web*, think about how a spider is made attractive. One of the best ways of making anything more attractive is to have it speak and express feelings.

8 Look at the animals names below.

lion

horse

butterfly

slug

chicken

panda

cat

sparrow

dog

badger

frog

ant

rat

peacock

whale

sea-urchin

cow

scorpion

chimpanzee

goldfish

a) Is it possible to arrange them in order of importance? There might be many different ways of thinking about importance: for example, how rare a species is it, how useful is it, how willing or unwilling would you be to allow it to be killed. Decide for yourself what is important.

b) If you feel that you cannot put them in order of importance, think of someone else who might put them in order: for example, someone wanting to make an animal adventure film, or someone deciding how money should be spent to protect different animals.

c) Discuss your list with others in the class. How much agreement is there? If you disagree with someone else's list, see if you can work out and explain why they put the animals in that order.

Let Sleeping Dogs Lie

The hut was well hidden, at the end of a long, dank and bush-covered track. In the half light of the evening, it was almost invisible, even when you were close up. At dusk, on a wet Wednesday night in October, it made a fairly spooky place to be. They approached along the river bank under cover of the gathering gloom.

It all began a week earlier when a small item in the local free newspaper caught Joseph's eye. It was a report on rumours that illegal dog fights were taking place in the area, but that so far RSPCA officers and the police had not managed to find the place. At lunchtime that day at school, Joseph had waved the paper under Christine's nose.

"Look, here's something real we could be doing. All this talk about animals, rights, ecology and so forth. Why don't we try and track down these dog fights and expose them? That would actually achieve something, wouldn't it?"

Gavin, ever one to look for an easy life, just laughed at him, but Michelle turned on him.

"Don't laugh Gavin. Somebody has to take a stand. Think what intelligent, friendly creatures dogs are. They've lived with human beings for thousands of years, and this is how we repay them. The people who like to see them tear each other to pieces can't be human!"

And somehow her enthusiasm and Joseph's goading got them all searching for the place where the fights might be held. It was Leila who proved to be the best detective. She found a place on one side of the town, where the river ran between banks of scrub, and there were bits of waste ground, smallholdings where a few animals were kept, interspersed with junk yards and rubbish tips. There were any number of sheds and barns where people might meet for illegal dog-fighting.

A week later, she gathered the group together and told them she thought she had found it. "There's a barn with some horrible noises coming out of it," she said. "I'm sure there's an animal in pain - I could hear it screaming and struggling. I couldn't get near yesterday because there's a barbed wire fence all round, and rough-looking men around all day. We must do something!" So they arranged to meet at eight o'clock and investigate further. Joseph agreed to bring a pair of heavy-duty wire cutters to get through the fence, and Christine knew where she could borrow a camera with a powerful flash. In their oldest clothes they crept along the river-bank towards the place Leila showed them.

"Are you sure we should be doing this?" said Pallavi, "It feels like breaking and entering - we could get into trouble!"

"Don't give up now," hissed Joseph "Think of those poor tortured animals. It's the people doing this who'll get in trouble. Are you sure this is the place, Leila?"

Just then their doubts were put to flight by the sound of a shrill animal scream, followed by a series of grunts, like a creature desperately trying to escape. Without more ado, Joseph cut the fence and they scrambled through as quickly as they could. The screams and squeals continued as they hunted through the dark, searching for the barn where the sounds came from. There were no sounds of people about, none of the shouting and roaring they had expected from a dogfight.

"Perhaps this is one of the victims, left to suffer," whispered Michelle to Gavin.

Eventually they found it. The shed was barred on the outside, but not locked. There were sounds of an animal struggling inside, but no sounds of people. Leaving Leila on watch outside, they lifted the latch and peered in. Gavin checked that there were no windows to show a light, and switched on his torch. In rows on the concrete floor along both sides of the shed, each in its own barred compartment, were six enormous pigs. At the end of the row one of them screamed and struggled, and they saw that it was fastened to the ground by a harness around its shoulders and a short length of chain. When they looked closer, they saw that each pig was in a similar harness, chained down, and although they were not in such distress as the sow at the end, they were chewing the bars, foaming at the mouth and rolling their eyes.

"Why?" gasped Michelle, her face white and her lips trembling. She had expected to be shocked, she had expected to see animals in distress, but this was so different from what she had expected, she didn't know how to handle it. "What's the matter with them?"

Grimly, Christine took out the camera, aimed it at the struggling pig, and took a series of flash photos. So intent were they on this that they didn't hear Leila's shout of alarm, until a more powerful torch than Gavin's shone from the doorway, and a voice full of authority called out,

"And just what do you think you are doing here?". They turned and saw a uniformed policeman, with another man behind him spluttering with rage. "Vandals! What are you doing to my sows! These are valuable animals - if you've hurt them I'll have your hides - the lot of you!"

Christine was at her best in this sort of situation. She drew herself up to her full height, took one step forward into the middle of the barn, and said in her clearest, coldest voice,

"Hurt them? We have done nothing but take photographs. Are you responsible for this - this outrage?"

"That's enough, young lady!" interrupted the policeman. "You're all of you on private property where you have no business to be. I'm going to have to take you down to the station and inform your parents."

It was a long, miserable and confusing evening. Their explanation was eventually accepted, and both police and parents believed that had genuinely been trying to expose an illegal activity. But they were left in no doubt that they had gone entirely the wrong way about it.

"You were lucky," said Gavin's dad a few days later. "If you really had stumbled on a dog-fighting ring, you'd quite likely be in hospital by now. As it is, all you did was annoy a perfectly respectable pig-breeder who had nothing to fear from the law."

"But . . . but . . ." stammered Gavin, "he was torturing them! You didn't see it! That sow was desperate!"

"I may not have seen it, but an official from the Ministry of Agriculture did. Mr. Barnsley who owns those pigs asked them to come round and clear his name, after the wild accusations you lot were making. Everything he is doing there is standard pig-raising practice, and perfectly legal. Apparently the sows only struggle like that for a few hours after they're put in the harness. They soon get used to it, and settle down to chewing the bars. And I don't understand why you're making such a fuss. It's only pigs we're talking about, not active animals like dogs or horses. Lying around is what they do all day anyway. It's not as if it was an active, friendly creature like a dog."

"Well," said Gavin doubtfully, "It doesn't seem natural to me. Those other pigs didn't look as if they had got used to it - they were just tired of struggling. I'm going to find out more. You get in trouble for leaving your dog chained up all the time."

---

i   **Attitude of Islam and Judaism to Pigs**

Both Islam and Judaism have clear laws about diet. Although there are many differences, both the Hebrew Bible and the Qur'an forbid the eating of pork or any product from a pig. Both faiths regard the pig as an unclean animal, and some Jews and Muslims have carried this further, to feel distaste for the animal itself.

Activities

1. Read the information about the attitude of Islam and Judaism to pigs. In the story, Joseph is Jewish and Leila is Muslim. Write a conversation that they might have had after they discovered that the animals suffering were pigs.

2. Read the information in chapter 8, page 71 about the natural behaviour of pigs. If you are not familiar with dogs, find books in the library about dogs and their nature and needs. Using this information, make a list of similarities and differences between dogs and pigs. Discuss your lists in class and try to compile an agreed list. You may find differences of opinion. Make a note of these.

3. Gavin's father suggested that different animals (in this case pigs and dogs) deserve or need different treatment. Do you agree? Explain why you agree or disagree.

4. Look at the information on page 71 about different laws for poultry compared with other caged birds. Why do you think the laws are different? Do you think there are good reasons for this?

5. Find books in the library about keeping dogs. From these, answer the following questions:
What activities does a dog need every day?
How much space does the average dog need?
What happens if a dog does not get enough company or exercise?
How should one care for a pregnant bitch?
How should one care for a bitch giving birth and her puppies?

6. Repeat the exercise above in relation to pigs.

7. A character in Shakespeare's play *Measure for Measure* says:
"And the poor beetle, that we tread upon,
In corporal sufferance [bodily suffering] finds a pang as great
As when a giant dies."
What do you think?

CHAPTER 6

Knowledge, Science and Technology

This chapter will explore some of the principles and moral considerations which should govern the pursuit of knowledge. It will look specifically at developments in relation to animals, such as selective breeding, genetic engineering and routine administering of drugs.

From *The Restaurant at the end of the Universe*
page 92-93

A large dairy animal approached Zaphod Beeblebrox's table, a large fat meaty quadruped of the bovine type with large watery eyes, small horns and what might almost have been an ingratiating smile on its lips.

'Good evening', it lowed and sat back heavily on its haunches, "I am the main dish of the day. May I interest you in parts of my body?" It harrumphed and gurgled a bit, wiggled its hind quarters into a more comfortable position and gazed peacefully at them.

Its gaze was met by looks of startled bewilderment from Arthur and Trillian, a resigned shrug from Ford Prefect and naked hunger from Zaphod Beeblebrox.

"Something off the shoulder perhaps?" suggested the animal, "braised in a white wine sauce?"

"Er, your shoulder?" said Arthur in a horrified whisper.

"But naturally my shoulder, sir," mooed the animal contentedly, "nobody else's is mine to offer."

Zaphod leapt to his feet and started prodding and feeling the animal's shoulder appreciatively.

"Or the rump is very good," murmured the animal. "I've been exercising it and eating plenty of grain, so there's a lot of good meat there." It gave a mellow grunt, gurgled again and started to chew the cud. It swallowed the cud again.

"Or a casserole of me perhaps?" it added.

"You mean this animal actually wants us to eat it?" whispered Trillian to Ford.

"Me?" said Ford, with a glazed look in his eyes, "I don't mean anything."

"That's absolutely horrible, "exclaimed Arthur, "the most revolting thing I've ever heard."

"What's the problem Earthman?" said Zaphod, now transferring his attention to the animal's enormous rump.

"I just don't want to eat an animal that's standing there inviting me to," said Arthur, "It's heartless."

"Better than eating an animal that doesn't want to be eaten," said Zaphod.

"That's not the point," Arthur protested. then he thought about it for a moment. "Alright," he said, "maybe it is the point. I don't care. I'm not going to think about it now. I'll just . . . er . . ."

. . . .

"I think I'll just have a green salad," he muttered.

"May I urge you to consider my liver?" asked the animal, "it must be very rich and tender by now, I've been force-feeding myself for months."

"A green salad," said Arthur emphatically.

"A green salad?" said the animal, rolling its eyes disapprovingly at Arthur.

"Are you going to tell me," said Arthur, "that I shouldn't have green salad?"

"Well," said the animal, "I know many vegetables that are very clear on that point. Which is why it was eventually decided to cut through the whole problem and breed an animal that actually wanted to be eaten and was capable of saying so clearly and distinctly. And here I am."
It managed a very slight bow.

"Glass of water please," said Arthur.

Douglas Adams, 1980, Pan Books

---

i Selective breeding and genetic engineering

Selective breeding of both plants and animals has been taking place ever since farming began. Farmers would select the best of their herd to breed from, using whatever characteristics they felt made a better animal - faster, larger, healthier, giving more milk, etc.

However, techniques developed in the last fifty years have dramatically increased the ability of stock breeders to select particular characteristics. The most common of these is artificial insemination, whereby one male can father vast numbers of offspring, without ever coming into contact with the females. Some people believe that this is wrong because of the unnatural way the animals are treated.

Another problem which arises is that animals can be bred for particular characteristics which are desirable for humans but which may affect the quality of life for the animals. Examples are cows which produce so much milk that their bodies cannot cope (see p.72), or dogs which are bred to have such flat

i continued

noses that they have difficulty in breathing. See also p.70 for breeding of broiler chickens.

Selective breeding uses the processes of natural reproduction, even if it harnesses them and uses them in highly technological ways. Genetic engineering uses science and technology in ways that go far beyond natural processes. Most importantly, it has never before been possible to exchange genes between unrelated species. Genetic engineering involves taking material from one species and artificially implanting it in another. At present, researchers have very little knowledge about the wider effects of such transfers.

Both selective breeding and genetic engineering have the danger that if large numbers of animals are produced from the same genetic stock, a disease or problem could affect all of them in the same way, and there would be no variety to provide some hope of resistance to disease. Researchers say that they are breeding for resistance to disease - but no-one knows what diseases may appear in the future.

Beliefs about the value of science

Islam

The Holy Prophet has said: 'The quest of knowledge is obligatory for every Muslim'.

The Holy Prophet has said 'Seek knowledge from the cradle to the grave'. There are many accounts of the sayings of the Prophet Muhammad which, like those above, emphasise the importance given in Islam to study and knowledge. Using one's God-given intelligence to find out more about the world that God made is seen as a religious activity - as indeed all actions of everyday life are part of living one's religion. But knowledge, science and technology are not regarded as ends in themselves, nor as being there to make people's lives more comfortable. Because human beings are regarded as God's Khalifah on earth (a Khalifah is one who acts or rules on behalf of another), the importance of science, like all knowledge, is that the more people know about the world that God created, the better they can live in the world in submission to God. (Islam means 'submission'). Because God is one, and created everything, all knowledge leads back to God, and all knowledge is interrelated. This means that any knowledge must be fitted into its proper place, and looked at in the light of other knowledge, especially knowledge about God.

Hindu

There are many ancient Indian scientific texts, especially medical texts, so science has an important place in Hindu thinking. But Hindus say that you have to be very careful about acquiring knowledge. Not all kinds of knowledge are of equal value, and some sorts of knowledge are even regarded as undesirable. Knowledge must be sought

i continued

for the right reasons, and scientific knowledge must always be balanced by spiritual knowledge. One of the most important Hindu scriptures, the Bhagavad Gita, describes one who has scientific knowledge but who does not surrender to God as 'one whose knowledge is stolen by illusion'. (7, 15). Knowledge which is only concerned with keeping the body comfortable is described as 'ignorant knowledge', or 'knowledge in darkness'.

There is a Hindu story about a demon who set out to mine all the gold in the earth. He was so powerful that no-one could stop him, and he dug deeper and deeper into the earth in his greedy passion for gold. Eventually he upset the balance of the earth, and it fell from its position in space until the god Vishnu restored its balance and put it back in its right place. Many Hindus believe that modern technology is upsetting the balance of the earth, and of nature, all for the sake of human greed.

Christian

Modern Western science grew out of Western Christian culture, but many Christians are now unhappy about the way science and technology have developed. Whereas many religions think of the natural world as being in some way the dwelling place of God, Christianity teaches that God is outside it and above it. Christians also believe that God put human beings in charge of the earth, and placed them above all other species. This has made it possible to investigate, cut up, and experiment with the natural world in a way that was not encouraged by other faiths and cultures.

At its best, Christian involvement in science was the studying of nature because it is a work of God and God loves it. But at times the idea of human authority over nature has overshadowed the idea of respect for nature, and Christians have felt justified in any kind of investigation in pursuit of knowledge.

Jewish

The book of Wisdom in the Hebrew Bible describes Wisdom as an aspect of God, and celebrates human learning, but always under God's guidance.

May God grant me to speak as he would wish
and express thoughts worthy of his gifts,
since he is the guide of Wisdom
since he directs the sages.
We are indeed in his hand, we ourselves and our words,
with all our understanding too, and our technical knowledge.
It was he who gave me true knowledge of all that is,
who taught me the structure of the world and the properties of the elements,
the beginning, end and middle of times,
the alternation of the solstices and the succession of the seasons
the revolution of the year and the positions of the stars,
the nature of animals and the instincts of wild beasts,
the powers of the spirits and the mental processes of humans,
the varieties of plants and the medicinal properties of their roots.
All that is hidden, all that is plain, I have come to know,
Instructed by Wisdom who designed them all.   *(Wisdom 7: 15-21)*

i continued

The Jews have always had a tradition of respect for study and learning. God's creation is good, as the book of Genesis states repeatedly in its account of creation, and therefore study of how the world works is good. But this does raise the question of how far it is allowable to change the created world, as is done to a limited extent in selective breeding, and much more clearly in genetic engineering. The book of Leviticus in the Bible give several different laws about not mixing things of different types, including "Do not mate different kinds of animals." This would seem to mean that genetic engineering of animals is forbidden.

Activities

1. Imagine for a moment that the story in this chapter could happen. Why do you think that the animal had been bred as it was? What were people looking for when they set out to breed it?

2. In the story, why is Arthur so upset at the thought of eating this animal? Do you agree with him? What would you do in his situation? Explain your reasons.

3. Still imagining that the story could happen some time in the future, do you think it was right to have bred the animal?

4. Make a collection of information about different breeds of dog. (Pictures, description of appearance, temperament, suitability for different circumstances etc.)
Take four breeds that are very different from each other, and for each one list four distinctive characteristics (for example, thick coat, short legs, friendly nature, likes to sleep a lot).
For each characteristic that you have listed, write down:
How does this benefit the dog?
How does this benefit its human owner?

When you think about benefits to humans, you should consider questions such as vanity and prestige, as well as practical benefits.

5. In groups, draw up
a). rules that you feel should regulate selective breeding of animals
b). rules that you feel should regulate genetic engineering of animals.

6. Some scientists and philosophers have discussed the possibility of breeding animals whose natural behaviour and desires have been altered, for example to breed naturally docile pigs and chickens which will not object to being kept in small enclosures, or chickens with much smaller wings so that they do not suffer so much in battery conditions. Take one of the religions described in the information box, and decide whether members of that faith would believe this is right.

Poor Cow

It seemed such an innocent idea at first. Pallavi and Michele had both decided to go into town to watch a cycle race zoom past. The cyclists were due to pass through the Town Hall square at about 11.30 a.m. on Saturday, so the two friends agreed to make a morning out of it and to meet to go shopping beforehand.

They arrived in the square about half an hour before the event was due to take place. People were already beginning to fill up the area and Pallavi and Michele had a bit of a struggle getting to a good spot. For about ten minutes they just chatted and watched the crowd. But then suddenly the clear path that had been created through the crowd for the cyclists to whizz down, was full of people rolling on the ground, followed almost immediately by policemen and women who leapt over the barriers.

"What on earth is going on?" asked Michele. Someone beside them said "Demonstrators by the look of them", and shrugged his shoulders. Pallavi and Michele looked at each other. Demonstrators! What on earth could they be demonstrating about? As if to answer their silent question, a voice shouting through a megaphone rose from the group being dragged off the road by the police.

"Stop the torture. Save the cows. Milk for us means suffering to animals." Then the megaphone was pulled from the woman's hands and she too was bundled out of the roadway.

Pallavi and Michele looked at each other again.

"What torture?" asked Pallavi. "Search me" said Michele. Before they could get any answer, a great cheer went up from the crowd and the first cyclists appeared. Over the next few minutes, the two friends were too busy enjoying the sight of lots of young men in very tight cycling shorts pedalling through the square!

As the crowd dispersed, Pallavi and Michele began to wander towards the bus station. Suddenly Michele realised that Pallavi was no longer with her. She had run across the road and was speaking to a woman Michelle had never seen before.

"What on earth has got into her?" wondered Christine, and hurried across to join them. As she arrived at her friend's side, the woman was saying,

"Yes, I was with them. My name's Anna. This race is sponsored by a major producer of milk and dairy foods. There's a group of us trying to wake people up to what milk really means these days."

"There's nothing wrong with milking cows, is there?" said Pallavi. "My dad tells me we should love cows like our own mother, because they give milk and butter and yogurt - it's their nature to give. That's why we Hindus don't kill them or eat them."

"Give!" snorted Anna, "you call it giving? It's more like slave labour! They're bred to give more milk than their udders can support, they're forced to have a calf every year - but they can't do the natural thing and feed their calf.

It's taken away from them after twenty four hours, so we can have all the milk. And, not content with that, people are talking of injecting them with hormones to make them 'give' even more milk. It's a nice cosy picture, the gentle cow happily giving her milk to the rosy-cheeked milkmaid, but it's a lie!"
Then she saw the look on Pallavi's face.

"I'm sorry, I didn't mean to shout at you. It's all new to you, and I can see it's a bit of a shock. Here, take one of these leaflets and read it at home."

On the bus journey home Pallavi was silent, and when she got home she went straight to her room and shut the door. She read the leaflet carefully, and then sat staring at the wall.

Then she got out her diary and began to write.

"I don't know what to do. I try to live a good life. I am a vegetarian because of what I believe. And we drink and use milk in so many ways. But now I know that there are terrible things done to make milk. I was happy before I knew. In some ways I wish I had never found out. What do I say to Mum and Dad? I am sure they don't know anything about all this. What am I going to do?"

i ## Hindus and Cow Protection

It is a central part of Hindu belief that all living beings, whether human, mammal, insect, or anything else, share the same universal spirit. Most Hindus are vegetarian for this reason, and their diet is based on grains and dairy products. In India, cows and oxen are extremely important for the life of a village, as the cows produce milk and the oxen work the fields and pull carts for transport. Hindus believe that in return for their milk and their labour, cows and bulls should be protected and cared for as members of the community. When they are old, they are not killed as in most commercial farms, but retired to pasture and cared for until they die naturally, just as one would a human member of the community.
ISKCON, the International Society for Krishna Consciousness, is engaged in extending this practice from India to many different parts of the world. They set up farms which aim to be self-sufficient and which rely on co-operation with cows and bulls. Many of these farms also take cows from commercial dairy farms who would have been sent for slaughter, and give them a 'retirement home' where they are cared for.

Islam and milking
No-one should over-burden an animal, for Allah forbids man to treat an animals in a way which would cause it unnecessary pain. Every animal is protected by Allah and the person who violates this protection violates the order of Allah. A man cannot even milk an animal at a time or in a way which would damage its young. This is because the milk belongs to the young animal. Moreover, before a Muslim comes to milk a cow, he is expected to cut his nails so that he does not unwittingly hurt her.
Mawil Y. Izzi Dien, 'Islamic Ethics and the Environment' in *Islam and Ecology* ed. Fazlun Khalid with Joanne O'Brien, Cassells/WWF 1992

Activities

1. Read the information about dairy cows in chapter 8, page 72 to find out more about what Pallavi has learnt. Imagine that Pallavi's mother calls her to come and eat a dish made with yogurt. What do you think Pallavi should do? For example, should she eat it or not? Should she tell her mother what she has learnt? Should she try and put it out of her mind?
Write, or act out, the scene between Pallavi and her mother.

2. Read the information on Islam and milking on page 61, and the information about dairy cows in chapter 8, page 72.
If Leila, who is a Muslim, had been with them, what would her reaction be?

3. Take one animal whose life is described in chapter 8.
a) Do you think that the application of science helps to make farm animals' lives better or worse?
b) If you think it makes lives better in general, are there circumstances where wrong use might make them worse? Or if you think it makes them worse in general, could the use of science be changed so as to make them better?

4. a) Read the information about dairy cows on page 72. List ways in which science has affected the life of the cows.
b) Read the information above on the attitude of different religions to science and learning. Take one faith, and suggest ways in which the cows' lives might be different if the principles of that faith were followed carefully. Would their lives be generally better or worse?

5. The following passage is from an information booklet about food production in Britain. Do you agree with it? Give your reasons. If there are a variety of opinions in the class, conduct a debate.
Farming in Britain is a success story. Tremendous developments in production, science and technology, machinery and livestock husbandry have created a highly successful industry in which under 3% of the population produce 80% of our necessary food that can be grown in this country.

6. Many people think that science and technology are the key to providing enough food to feed everyone in the world. Where do you think scientists should be concentrating their attention if this is to happen? (For example, animal breeding, plant breeding, new sources of food, pest control, etc.). Make a class list of possible areas of research, and vote for the most important.

7. Some people suggest that scientists are not responsible for the effects and uses of the knowledge that they find out. Do you think this is true? Who ought to take the responsibility?

CHAPTER 7

Death

All living things die. Mayflies live only one day. Some giant tortoises live for a hundred years or more. But - eventually - everything dies. Many of the stones and rocks of our planet are made up of the skeletons of billions of creatures who died millions of years ago.

Many living things die to provide food for other creatures. Flies die in spiders' webs, worms die in the beaks of birds. Mice and voles die in the jaws of cats or the talons of owls and hawks.

Human beings are part of this same natural world. We too die, and many of us eat other creatures. The world's faiths and other belief systems have differing views about whether this is right or necessary, and about what death means.

To Live or to Die

(A Hindu story)
Savarjna the wise man was once on a journey. On the road he passed four travellers, one after another. The first traveller was a prince, dressed in fine silk and riding in comfort. It was Savarjna's habit to give a blessing to everyone he passed, so he said,

"May you live a long life, for after this life you will have to pay for all the selfish pleasures you are now enjoying."

Next came a student of the scriptures who was living a very austere life of fasting for the sake of spiritual advancement.

"May you die soon," Savarjna blessed, "so that you can go to the heavenly planets and enjoy the results of your sacrifice."
The third traveller was a butcher, with his clothes stained with blood and the carcase of an animal in his cart.

"It is best that you neither live nor die," exclaimed Savarjna. "Your present life is hellish, and your future life will also be hellish because those who live by killing others will have to suffer in the planets of hell."

Finally Savarjna met a devotee of Krishna, absorbed in chanting the names of God.

"You may either live or die," he said, "For you it makes no difference: in this life you are happy, and in your next life you will be happy, because you live always in the presence of God."

(adapted from Ranchor Prime, 'Hindu Educational Values' in Interlink Final Report, WCC, 1990)

---

i   **Hindu attitudes to death**

The principle of reincarnation is explained in chapter 4, page 40. Because Hindus believe that all living creatures embody the same universal spirit, they regard taking the life of another creature as an extremely serious thing to do. It should certainly never be done for one's own selfish pleasure. But the Bhagavad Gita, the best-loved of the Hindu scriptures, is a discussion of the dilemma of a young prince Arjuna who is hesitating about fighting a battle in which he knows many people will be killed. The God Krishna reassures him: You are mourning for what is not worthy of grief. Those who are wise lament neither for the living nor for the dead. (2.11)

One who has taken his birth is sure to die and, after death, one is sure to take birth again. Therefore, in the unavoidable discharge of your duty, you should not lament. (2.27)

I have already slain these men, you are only an instrument. (11.33) (Quoted from The Essential Teachings of Hinduism, ed. Kerry Brown, Rider, 1988)

Krishna is saying that since death is inevitable for everyone, any individual death is of no great importance. Each person should concentrate on fulfilling their own duty.

Activities

1. Look at the information on reincarnation in Chapter 4, p. 40, and information box above. Why do you think Savarjna regarded his words to the second traveller, the student of the scriptures, as a blessing rather than a curse?

2. a) If you were making a good wish for a baby's future, would you wish him or her a long life, a happy life, or a life which does good to other people?
b) Would you wish the same for an animal?
c) What wishes would you make for the person's or the animal's death?

The Hare on the Moon

The Buddha who is all-knowing has been reborn on Earth many times in many forms - as a man, as an animal and as a spirit. In the Jataka book there are stories about 550 of his lives. This is one of them.
Long ago the future Buddha was born as a hare and lived in a forest. He

had three wise friends, monkey, jackal and otter.

The animals all led good lives and Hare reminded them not to eat on the holy fast-days and to give food to whoever asked them for it.

One day, the animals were seeking food as usual. Otter caught a fish, Jackal caught some meat and Monkey found three mangoes. But Hare lay in his hole feeling too upset to go and eat his grass. He had just realised he had nothing to give.

"What can I do if someone asks me for a gift of food?" he thought. "All I have is grass and that's no good to anyone but a hare."

Then a solution came to him. If someone asked him for food, he would give up his own body to feed them. So unselfish was this thought that it reached Sakra on his throne in Heaven.

Sakra decided to see for himself if Hare was truly noble. He went down to Earth and took the shape of a holy man, called a Brahman. First, he went to otter and asked him for food. Otter offered him his fish. Then he went to Jackal and Monkey and they offered him meat and mangoes. Sakra said thank you but did not take their food.

Next, he went to Hare. Hare was overjoyed to have the chance to give. "Brahman," he said, "today I will give as I have never given before". He told the holy man to gather wood and light a fire. When the fire was crackling brightly, Hare threw himself into it. But the flames around him were as cool as the air in his burrow. He stood on the blazing logs and looked at Sakra in surprise.

"Brahman, what has happened to your fire?" he asked.

"I am Sakra", said Sakra "I have come down from Heaven to test your generosity and you have shown me it is as endless as the universe."

Sakra tucked the hare under one arm and picked up a mountain with the other.

"Wise hare, your virtue will be seen by all creation until the end of this world cycle" he said.

Sakra squeezed the mountain and used its juice as ink to draw an outline of the hare on the moon. Then he put Hare back down in a field of grass and returned to Heaven. And that is why there is now a hare on the left hand edge of the moon.

i   **Buddhism and meat-eating**

Buddhism teaches compassion for all creatures, as well as urging a gradual detachment from desires, especially desires for luxuries. Because of this, Buddhist teaching says that avoiding meat is the ideal, and people should try to aim for this gradually. Chinese Buddhism recognises several different stages. In the first stage, a Buddhist would not eat meat on the first and the fifteenth day of each month. As a second stage they would also avoid it on religious festivals. Buddhist monks are totally vegetarian.

The story shows that, while meat-eating is not regarded as an evil in itself, it is extremely costly to the animal concerned!

Buddhism has had a great influence on the culture of Japan, and a hundred years ago, the Japanese ate virtually no meat. When an animal was killed for food, it was not done lightly, and a prayer was said asking that the creature be released from agony, that its soul would pass peacefully into the next life and become a Buddha. However, in recent years, many Japanese have become meat-eaters, and Japan has been an outspoken defender of the right to hunt and eat whales. A ceremony is still held each year to pray for the souls of the whales that have been killed, but it is organised by the largest whaling company.

Activities

1. In chapter 3. page 25, we imagined what prayers an animal might pray. What prayer do you think the hare in the story might have prayed before sacrificing its life?

2. Compare this story with the extract from *The Restaurant at the End of the Universe* in ch. 6, p. 55-56. Each animal is quite willing to die to provide food. Is there a difference in their attitudes?
Choose one of the stories, and write a poem about how it makes you feel.

3. There are different beliefs about how people will be judged at the end of their life or the end of time. Often an epitaph or obituary gives an indication of what the dead person saw as most important in their life, or what their friends thought was most important.
a) Write an obituary for yourself, concentrating on what you care about, for example, 'she was someone who loved sports'; 'he was a great reader'. Include as many things as possible that are important to you.
b) Then do the same thing for each of the following animals: how would you sum up their life in terms of what was important about them?
    i. a domestic animal, such as a hamster, cat or dog;
    ii. a farm animal such as a cow or hen;
    iii. a wild animal.
As far as possible, choose animals whose life you are familiar with.

4. Many societies that live by hunting have a prayer or a ceremony to ask forgiveness of the animals that they will kill. Even if you do not eat meat, virtually all of us living in Britain have a lifestyle that in some way threatens the life of other creatures: houses and roads destroy animals' habitats; pollution from transport poisons the environment, etc. And yet it is difficult to live any other

way. Design a ceremony which recognises the suffering that our life imposes on other creatures, and asks their forgiveness.

Rabbi Judah the Patriarch

The story is told that one day this Rabbi saw a calf being taken to be slaughtered. It ran to him and nestled its head in his robe and whimpered. He said to it, "Go! this is what you were created for!"

But because he had no mercy on the calf, heaven decreed that he should suffer from toothache for many years. He was eventually healed when he saw his housekeeper about to kill some young mice. He said to her, "Let them go free, for it is written that 'His mercies are over all his works'."

i   Jewish Laws about Slaughter

Jewish rules about how animals should be killed for meat were developed over many years, based on instructions in the Bible about how animals should be treated, and were finally written down in the Talmud, as a summary of the discussions of respected Rabbis (teachers). The rules are rooted in the principle that the animal should suffer as little as possible.

The slaughtering of animals for food is not just a job in Jewish society. It is also a religious function, and cannot be undertaken by just anyone. The shochet, as he is called in Hebrew, must be a man of good physical health and strength, a religious man whose character is recognised as responsible and good. He must also have studied the Torah, the Jewish Bible, in detail, as well as the discussions of Rabbis since the Torah was written. And he must have learned his trade with a qualified shochet before he is allowed to set up on his own. Moses ben Maimon, one of the most famous of Jewish thinkers, who lived in Spain in the twelfth century, summed up the principle as follows:

"Since the need of procuring food necessitates the slaying of animals, the law lays down that the death of the animal should be the easiest."

Opinions vary as to whether the Jewish method of slaughter is in fact the most humane available. With a single clean stroke the animal's windpipe, jugular vein and gullet are severed, and the animal loses consciousness almost immediately. This is why the health and strength of the shochet is so important, as a hesitant or weak stroke would not produce this effect.

It is important for Jews to remember the reason for the traditional method of slaughter, and to consider the conditions in which the animal has been kept, transported, and prepared for slaughter as being just as important as the method of killing itself.

Islamic laws about slaughter

The most important point about the slaughter of animals in Islam is that it should be done in the name of God. The phrase 'In the name of God' is pronounced over the animal just before slaughtering it. This is not intended to be just a form of words. It implies that the animal is being killed for a purpose which God allows (that is, for necessary

i   Buddhism and meat-eating

food). It also implies that the act must take place in a way which God allows, without unnecessary suffering.

The Prophet Muhammad laid great stress on the need to prevent both physical and mental suffering for animals: he is reported as saying that the knife should be well sharpened, but he once rebuked a man who was sharpening his knife in the presence of the animal, as this would cause it mental suffering: "Do you intend to inflict death on the animal twice - once by sharpening the knife within its sight, and once by cutting its throat?" He also forbade slaughtering an animal in the presence of other animals, and was once angry because a man refused a drink to a thirsty sheep which he was about to kill. On another occasion he was angry because an animal was being roughly handled before slaughter. The traditional method of muslim slaughter is similar to that of Judaism, for the same reasons. Muslims disagree about whether modern methods of slaughter, such as stunning before the animal is killed, are permissible for them.

Activities

1. If you had been Rabbi Judah the Patriarch in the story, what would you have done:
a) about the calf?
b) about the mice?

2. Imagine that you are in charge of a government department concerned with regulations about killing animals for meat. You have wide-ranging powers, and you are governing a country in which some people eat meat and others do not. There are people of many different religions in your country. In groups, draw up rules. Consider such questions as:
a) Are you going to allow meat-eating at all?
b) Do you want to control the number of animals that can be killed?
c) Do you want to control how, where and when the animals are killed?
d) Do you want to make rules about how the animals are treated before they are killed?
e) How much freedom are you going to give people to follow their own conscience?

3. Compare your regulations with the information given in chapter 8, p. 73-74. Do you think that British and EU regulations should be changed?

4. 'Since the need of procuring food necessitates the slaying of animals. . .'
These words are quoted from Moses ben Maimon in the information above. In groups, discuss:
a) Do you think it is true that in some situations animals must be killed for humans to have sufficient food?
b) In what other ways do human beings threaten the life of other species? (For example, by destroying their habitat, or polluting the environment)
c) Suggest two or three simple things that you, or people like you, could do in order to make less threat to other species.
Pool these ideas as a class.

CHAPTER 8

Farming Information

Battery eggs

We may have cheap eggs today, but hens pay dearly to produce them. A battery cage measures approximately 45 x 50 x 35 centimetres and is used to hold up to five birds - not very large when compared with their 80cm wingspan. Under the Welfare of Battery Hen Regulations (1987), cages should allow at least 450 sq.cm. floor space per bird (about the size of a sheet of A4 paper), when four or more birds are kept in one cage. Life in a battery cage means that hens are unable to move around easily, stretch their wings, perch, dustbathe or lay their eggs in a nest.

Hens need to have sufficient exercise. In natural conditions hens stretch their wings and flap them. They walk, run when required and fly up to and off their perches. All these behaviours are made impossible by lack of space. Wing flapping is necessary for good hen welfare. In one study, hens in percheries flapped 1.9 times per hour and flew twice in every 5 hours. In the cage, hens can neither flap nor fly. The cage's low ceilings also make certain head movements impossible. The EC Directive specifies a minimum height of 40 cm. over 65% of the cage area and 35 cm. over the rest; yet 25% of a hen's head movements take place above 40 cm.

Compassion In World Farming

In this broiler unit, chickens are packed so densely they can barely move

Hens need to perform certain foraging movements. In natural conditions hens spend much time scratching and pecking at the earth, looking for grubs and seeds to eat. In

Compassion In World Farming

Battery hens live in conditions that are unnatural and overcrowded

the cage a hen is unable to move around to forage and there is no material to scratch or peck at. This is made worse by the fact that the food provided is quickly eaten, whereas feeding activities normally occupy up to 50% of the hen's time.

Studies have shown that dust-bathing is also a very important activity for the hens, and that if they cannot dust-bathe, they are far more likely to peck the feathers of other hens. In the cage there is no dust to bathe in. Caged birds can, however, be seen performing the dustbathing movements, showing that the instinct is still strong. In natural conditions hens will build a nest in which to lay their eggs in privacy and comfort. Nest building is a fairly complex activity. It involves gathering material, transporting it and then constructing the nest. In the cage nest building is impossible, and hens can often be seen making nest building movements with no material.

Denied the freedom to behave naturally, battery cage hens will often turn on each other. Feather pecking is a serious problem which can, in some instances, lead to cannibalism and death. In order to prevent this, battery hens (and hens in alternative systems) are often debeaked. Debeaking is carried out by removing up to a third of the upper part of the beak with a hot blade. This process is very painful and studies have shown that it can result in long-term discomfort.

Free-range hens

These may be kept indoors with straw or litter and perches, but they must also have access to an outdoor area which must be mainly covered with vegetation. If well run, this system allows birds to behave in a more natural way. However, problems can still arise when too many birds are kept in too small an area. Legally, a stocking density of up to 1,000 birds per hectare can qualify as a free range system but many campaigners believe that 375 birds per hectare should be the maximum.

Egg labelling

The labelling of eggs in the shops is not designed to draw our attention to the facts about their production. Battery eggs, for example, are usually labelled as 'Fresh Farm Eggs' or 'Country Fresh', or similar, and a recent survey has shown that consumers are very confused by such labels. When interviewed, many people said that they bought free range eggs, but in fact they were buying battery eggs. Under EC regulations, eggs do not have to be labelled as coming from caged hens.

Broiler chickens

Chickens bred for meat, rather than for eggs, are known as broiler chickens. Most people's taste is for plenty of tender meat, so the birds have been bred to grow a great deal of muscle very fast, so that they can be slaughtered while they are still young and tender. Modern broiler fowl grow to the desired weight in just six weeks - about half the time it took 30 years ago. This has been achieved through selective breeding, but it has created huge health and welfare problems for the birds.

They often put on weight so fast that their young skeletons cannot support it, and they develop leg problems so that they can hardly walk. They may spend a great deal of their time resting on their breast on the litter (woodshavings/straw) they are kept on, which may be full of chicken droppings which contains amonia which burns their skin. In the worst cases, they may be unable to reach food and water.

The vast majority are reared in intensive units which can hold tens of thousands of birds. Chicks are placed in these large, windowless sheds at a few days old.

There are also problems for the adult birds. The majority of the birds, of course, do not reach adulthood, as they are slaughtered before this stage. But some have to be kept for breeding purposes, and their tendency to put on weight does not go away with adulthood. If allowed to feed as they wish, they would grow so large that they could not survive, so the birds that are to be kept for breeding are kept permanently hungry to prevent them growing too large. Selective breeding has created their desire to eat and put on weight, but it has not found a way to satisfy this desire without killing them.

Laws about caged birds

Section 8, subsection (1) of the Wildlife and Countryside Act 1981 states that: "If any person keeps or confines any bird whatever in any cage or other receptacle which is not sufficient in height, length or breadth to permit the bird to stretch its wings freely, he shall be guilty of an offence and be liable to a special penalty."
The following paragraph states that "Subsection (1) does not apply to poultry".

Natural behaviour of pigs

Pigs are very intelligent animals - at least as intelligent as dogs. If allowed to follow their natural instincts, they live in family groups near woodland. They use their sensitive snouts to root out tasty pieces to eat. Pigs are very clean animals. If they are given good conditions to live in, they will agree on a toilet area, and will not dirty the rest of their living space.

When a sow is about to give birth, she usually has a period of intense activity, finding straw or other bedding material and gathering it and pawing it to make a nest. In the twenty hours before her piglets are born, a sow who can roam freely may travel a total distance of 30 km. making her nest.

If the piglets are allowed to suckle for as long as they like, they will wean themselves naturally at 9-20 weeks old. But many piglets are taken from the sow at 3-4 weeks. Piglets are energetic and curious animals, and spend time exploring their surroundings, rooting in the ground or in straw. If they have no opportunity to do this, they often chew each other's tails, or show other sorts of stressed behaviour.

Sow stalls and farrowing crates

Until recently, about half of Britain's sows (there are 800,000 breeding sows in the UK) were kept in what are known as dry sow stalls and tethers. This close confinement frustrates the pig's natural behaviour and even prevents her from turning around. The cramped conditions commonly cause lameness, sores, hip problems and unnatural habits such as bar-biting. A CIWF Trust report prepared by Dr Baxter of the Centre for Rural Buildings, and published in 1986, concluded that close confinement of sows caused severe distress and that they reacted to this confinement in ways which closely resembled the development of chronic psychiatric disorders in humans. Because of this report and the campaign which followed it, a law has been passed phasing out sow stalls in the UK.

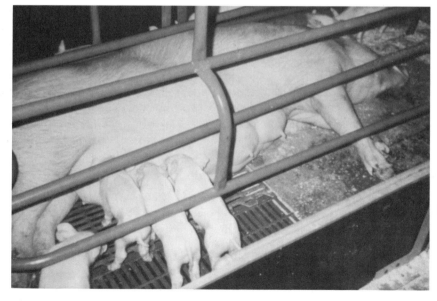

Compassion In World Farming

This sow suckles her piglets but her movement is severely limited by the bars of the farrowing crate

A few days before they are due to give birth, sows are moved into their farrowing accommodation - a narrow metal crate which is said to protect the new-born piglets from being trampled or rolled on by their mother. A sow would naturally become very active at this time and build a large nest of twigs, grasses and leaves. Within the restrictions of the farrowing crate this is, of course, impossible, and the sow is reduced to gnawing and pawing at the bars. More humane indoor farrowing systems are already in use and more are under development.

Conditions of pig raising

Piglets are usually weaned when they are 3 to 4 weeks old, and moved on for further fattening in a variety of systems. The flat-deck system consists of a darkened and environmentally-controlled house containing rows of single-tiered metal pens, usually with slatted floors. The pens are densely packed with 10-30 weaner pigs in each pen. With no bedding provided this is a barren environment. The cage system holds approximately ten piglets per cage in two or three tiers. This system has been condemned by the Farm Animal Welfare Council. The other type of accommodation used is the kennel system. The solid-floored kennel may have an outdoor verandah with perforated floor to allow the droppings to be carried away.

Dairy cows

Seeing dairy cows grazing in a green pasture, most people would assume that these animals, led a contented, natural life. Sadly, the reality is somewhat different and the modern dairy cow is a grossly overworked animal. At the age of 2, a dairy cow will be having her first calf. The calf will be taken away from its mother after 24 hours so that all the milk can be used for humans. A modern cow produces up to 50 litres of milk a day - 10 times as much as her calf would have drunk had it been left to feed from her. Between six and nine weeks later she will be made pregnant again - in 60% of cases by artificial insemination. She will then be milked for 10 months before her udder is given a rest in the last few weeks before her next calf is born.

The double burden of pregnancy and milk production is not normally inflicted on any mammal, and is likely to be one of the reasons for the cow's tendency to disease. This constant strain on the cow regularly leads to the painful infection known as mastitis. Mastitis causes inflammation of the udder and teats. Many dairy cows also become lame due to a combination of bad flooring and unsuitable food fed to them when they are kept inside over the winter. Cows can easily live into their twenties, but most dairy cows are sent for slaughter at about five years old.

Genetic engineering techniques have also been used to produce commercial quantities of a cattle growth hormone called BST - bovine somatotropin. The use of BST is controversial, even within the farming community. When injected into dairy cows, BST can increase milk production by between 10 and 20% - despite the fact that cows may already be being worked up to and beyond their natural capacity. CIWF is opposed to the use of BST and has campaigned vigorously against its use since experiments were first carried out. Research has shown that cows injected with BST also suffer more reproductive problems, painful swellings on injection sites, up to 35% increase in the incidence of mastitis and a generally poorer body condition.

Veal calves

Most of the male calves born to dairy cows are sold to be reared for veal. Until recently, many young calves were reared in small crates, kept in darkness and fed on a low-iron liquid diet to produce the pale flesh sold as white veal. The liquid-only diet denies them roughage and prevents normal development of their multiple stomach system. At six months they are slaughtered. However, in 1990, following a major campaign by Compassion in World Farming, the 'veal crate' system of rearing calves was outlawed in the UK, although it is still used in other EU countries and elsewhere.

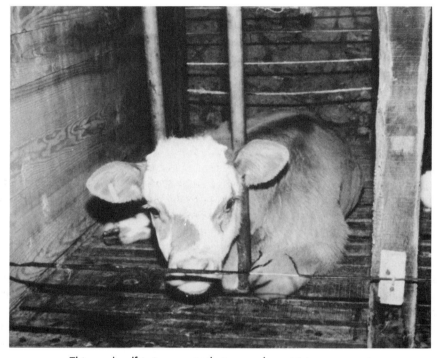

This veal calf is in a crate that severely restricts movement

Since 1990, calves in the UK have been kept in an alternative system. This system allows for the calves to be kept in groups where they have access to roughage and bedding. The calves are fed on demand from automatic machines which deliver milk replacer via artificial teats. This system does at least allow the calves freedom of movement and the opportunity to behave in a more natural manner.

Despite the lead taken by the UK government, there is no EC-wide ban on the veal crate. In 1993 approximately 500,000 calves were exported from the UK to the continent with most ending up in veal crates, mainly in the Netherlands and France.

Slaughter

Approximately 600 million broiler chickens and 34 million turkeys are slaughtered annually in the UK. Birds are tightly packed into crates to be taken away for slaughter. Having had little or no exercise, their leg bones are very brittle and one study found that almost a third of battery hens had suffered broken bones by the time they arrived at their final destination. It is also estimated that between one and two million broiler chickens die each year on the journey to the slaughterhouse.

Poultry are taken from their transport crates and hung upside down by their legs from shackles on a moving line. The birds' heads and chest are then trailed through an electrified water bath which is designed to stun them. The chickens then move on to automatic neck cutters. Death is caused by loss of blood. Birds then pass into a tank of scalding water to loosen the feathers before plucking. In 1993, the CIWF Trust produced a report which showed that a significant number of birds were not being stunned adequately and that the majority did not have their necks cut properly. This means that many birds are in danger of recovering consciousness as they slowly bleed to death and that some may even be alive when entering the scalding tank.

In 1993, 2,000,000 sheep and lambs were exported from the UK to other EU countries. They were sent directly for slaughter or for further fattening before slaughter. There is much stress involved in loading and unloading; being packed tightly together and experiencing extremes of temperature on what can be a long, exhausting journey. There is documented evidence to show that such animals regularly travel more than 24 hours without food, rest or water, and in one case for no less than 59 hours.

Regulations for slaughter

New EC hygiene and inspection regulations have meant that the number of slaughterhouses in the UK has virtually halved in the last few years. But in general these regulations have been to do with hygiene rather than animal welfare, and the smaller number of slaughterhouses means that many animals have to be transported much longer distances, causing greater stress.

The law states that animals must be stunned before they are killed, except in the special case of religious slaughter (see page 67). They must be made "instantaneously insensible to pain until death supervenes." Death is actually caused by loss of blood when the animal's throat is cut. There is evidence to show that although very quick, this is a very painful process if the animal is conscious at the time. Unfortunately, there have been many cases of animals not being correctly stunned, or not slaughtered quickly enough, so that they regain consciousness before they die.

These mistakes often happen because the staff at the slaughterhouse are not properly trained, or are under pressure to get through a certain amount of work. In particular, some slaughterhouse staff are paid on a piecework basis, by which they are paid according to how many animals they have slaughtered, rather than by the hour. This means they are much more likely to ignore the welfare needs of the animals.

CHAPTER 9

Action

This chapter will give more detailed information about what you can do about some of what you have learnt, if you so wish. Names and addresses of organisations, as well as which authorities are responsible for which aspect of animal welfare, are in the Appendix, page 92.

A Jewish tradition describes the efforts that Noah made on behalf of the animals in the ark. It was not sufficient just to have built the ark and brought pairs of the animals on board. They had to be cared for, and that is not easy: "Throughout those twelve months, Noah and his sons did not sleep, because they had to feed the animals, the beasts and the birds." (Tanhuma, 58, 9, quoted in Aubrey Rose, *Judaism and Ecology*, p.59)

Other people today follow Noah's example, working to help animals. At the end of this chapter there are addresses of several animal welfare and other organisations.

Compassion in World Farming is the leading farm animal welfare organisation in Europe. It campaigns against all farm animal cruelties and as well as making direct appeals to the public for support, spends a lot of time lobbying politicians, both at Westminster and, increasingly, at the European Parliament. CIWF has also organised demonstrations against specific abuses – from battery cages and live animal exports to veal crates and fur farming to name just a few. CIWF has around 12,000 members and over 3,000 young supporters.

This book has been prepared for Compassion in World Farming Trust, the educational wing of CIWF (address below), which can provide further information on many of the issues raised in the book, as well as videos, slides and speakers.

Most new farm animal welfare legislation and regulations now emanate from the European Commission in Brussels. MP's and MEP's of all major political parties have expressed concern about farm animal welfare. CIWF meets regularly with parliamentary representatives to discuss current issues; provides detailed information for questions and debates and participates in high level meetings at the European Commission and with Ministry officials in the UK.

CIWF's constant lobbying, protests and petitions do work. In recent years three important new laws have been passed in the UK Parliament. The first outlawed the keeping of calves in veal crates. More recently, CIWF initiated a Private Member's Bill with Sir Richard Body MP to outlaw the practice of keeping sows in sow stalls or tethering them to the floor. The provisions of the Bill were adopted by the Government as The Welfare of Pigs Regulations 1991. This new law means that all existing stalls and tethers will have to be phased out by the end of 1998. These are real measures which mean that thousands of animals will have improved living conditions and suffer less pain and stress. CIWF also worked closely with Sir Richard Body to secure the passage through Parliament of the Welfare of Animals at Slaughter Act (1991). This gives the government new regulation-making powers designed to reduce suffering at slaughter. In 1994 another law made regulations against sending very young lambs to market.

As individuals we can all make a stand by boycotting cruelly-produced farm products. There is an increasing awareness among consumers of farm animal cruelty and producers and retailers are now responding by offering "cruelty-free" and "welfare friendly" products. Personal choice ranges from opting for free-range and organically produced meat and dairy produce, to becoming a vegetarian or vegan (not eating meat, fish, eggs or any animal products).

There are ways to avoid the cruelties involved in modern farming. CIWF is not against farming, but it is against suffering. Over the last 25 years progress has been made in making people aware of this. This book has given some examples of the different ways in which people think about animals, and your own way of thinking will probably be different again. We are asking you to think about some of these issues rather than ignoring them, and to encourage other people to think about them too.

Here are some examples of what you might do if you feel that any or all of the food available in our shops involves unacceptable suffering.

Changing what you eat

You would need to discuss these changes with whoever is responsible for buying food in your household. Some of the changes we suggest (such as free-range eggs) cost more than you may be paying at the moment. Some of them (such as soya mince) cost less. See if you can come to an agreement. Some of the suggestions below involve taking extra trouble, for example to find out where to buy meat from an organic supplier (are you prepared to find out?) or a longer trip to a specialist shop (will you do some of the shopping?).

• Never buy 'white veal' (see chapter 8, p.71)

• If buying milk or meat, try to find an organic supplier whose welfare standards are high. Some supermarkets are beginning to stock meat and milk which has been produced in more humane ways.

• Try using soya milk and soya mince

- Think about eating less meat, milk products and eggs. If you are thinking of cutting these out of your diet altogether, you will need to make other changes in what you eat to make sure you get all the nutrients you need. These changes are quite easy once you get used to them, and there are many good vegetarian and vegan recipe books now available to help you.

- **Making your voice heard**
  If you have strong opinions about an issue, you should tell others about them.
- Write to an organisation concerned with animals or farming telling them why you agree with them;

- Write to an organisation telling them why you disagree with them;

- Write to a government department or your MP at Westminster or your MEP at the European Parliament, Rue Belliard 97-113, 1040 Brussels, Belgium, saying why a law should be changed (or not changed);

- If you are a member of a religious organisation such as a church or synagogue, encourage other members of your faith to think about how their food is produced, and whether this is in line with their beliefs.

- Some large food shops and supermarkets control the way their goods are produced at every stage: some even own the farms. Write to them to tell them how you want your food to be produced.

- **Telling other people**
  As well as just talking to people, there are various ways to put your point of view across. Here is an examples:

1. a) Using card or paper, make a model of a battery cage. The dimensions are given in chapter 8, page 69.
b) Take this model to people who are not studying this book (for example, show it in the corridor at break-time) and ask them 'How many hens do you think could be kept in this cage?'. Make it clear that the hens spend all their time in the cage. Make a note of their answers.
c) Tell them that five hens spend their whole life in a cage this size, and write down their reactions.
3. a) Measure the armspan of several different people in the class, and calculate the average. Then calculate what size a 'people battery' cage would be:
a= armspan x 46cm /76cm; b= armspan x 51cm/76cm
a x b = dimensions of cage.
(To check your calculations, a typical adult measurement is 96 x 107 cm.)
b) Measure out an area in the classroom this size and enclose it with chairs or tables. Ask five people to stand inside it.
c) Ask these people:
      Can you sit down?
      How would you sleep?
      How long could you spend like this?

CHAPTER 10

Assemblies

Many of the issues raised in this book are of far wider relevance than a simple focus on animals and the way we treat them. In many cases the specific work that the students have done on animals can form the focus of an assembly led by the class, and they can put forward their own conclusions. In other cases we make suggestions for building on some of the work they have done, or highlighting a general issue in an assembly that is mainly teacher-led. The assemblies given here loosely follow the chapters of the book, but one or two chapters do not lend themselves to assembly work. These are suggestions about how the work in the rest of the book might contribute to assemblies. No doubt you will find other ways.

1. More questions than answers

Purpose
To validate the asking of questions, even when answers may be hard to find.

Preparation
Decorate the hall with a large question mark, or with several scattered about.

Ask students to suggest various 'hard' or 'unanswerable' questions, some serious, such as 'what are we here for?', 'what is the origin of the world?', 'why do people suffer?', etc., some light-hearted, such as 'How long is a piece of string?', 'where do all the odd socks go?'

Assembly
Start with the children taking it in turns to ask their questions.

Alternatively, tell the following story:
A little boy and his father were sitting on a bus. The boy turned to his father and asked,
"Dad, what makes the bus go?"
"I don't really know, son."
A few minutes later, the boy piped up again:
"Dad, why does rain fall?"
"Well, son, I don't really know."
"Dad, why is that man running down the road?"
"I couldn't say."
"Dad, where does the sun go at night?"
"I'm not sure."
"Dad, Dad?"
"What is it?"
"Do you mind me asking all these questions?"
"Why no, son! If you never asked questions you'd never learn anything!"

Use the passage on page 9, headed 'More questions than Answers' to talk about the value of questioning.
If the students have done activity 1 on page 9, use some of their poems.

To sing
From *Alleluya*
31 Blowing in the wind
34 Can't help but wonder

Reading
The Rig Veda Creation Hymn (Penguin Classics) translation by Wendy Doniger O'Flaherty

1. There was neither non-existence nor existence then; there was neither the realm of space nor the sky which is beyond. What stirred? Where? In whose protection? Was there water, bottomlessly deep?

6. Who really knows? Who will here proclaim it? Whence was it produced? Whence is this creation? The gods came afterwards, with the creation of this universe. Who then knows whence it has arisen?

7. Whence this creation has arisen - perhaps it formed itself, or perhaps it did not - the one who looks down on it, in the highest heaven, only he knows - or perhaps he does not know.

2.What are we like?

Purpose

To allow reflection on the good and bad in human beings, and our effect on the world.

Preparation

Ask the students to collect newspaper headlines highlighting either the good that people do in the world, or the harm they do, covering as wide a variety as possible of different activities.

Then ask them jointly to write a prayer or meditation based on the contrast between these headlines, quoting as far as possible from the newspapers.

Assembly

Ask the question, 'What does it mean to be human?' and ask the students to read out some of their contrasting headlines.

Readings

Psalm 8

Job 38 (some parts of this are quoted on page 15-16)

Prayer

Use the meditation written by the students.

Hymn

Now join we, to praise the Creator (*Hymns Ancient and Modern New Standard* no. 500)

Although this is normally a harvest hymn, it underlines the contrast between the good and bad in the world, and can be used at any time.

From *Come and Praise*

1 Morning has broken

9 Fill your hearts with joy and gladness

10 God who made the earth

11 For the beauty of the earth

16 When God made the garden of creation

73 When your father made the world

3. What's the use of animals?

Preparation

Ask the students to prepare to perform one or more of the plays written in activity 2, page 21

Prepare one or more of the prayers written in activity 1, page 25

Assembly

Use the story 'Heaven's Provision' on page 20 to introduce the question.

Then ask the students to perform one or more of the plays written in activity 2, page 21

Ask the assembly to think about the question 'What are animals for?'

Prayer

Introduce and read *The Donkey* from page 24

and/or

ask the students to read one or more of the prayers from activity 1, page 25

Hymn

From *Come and Praise*

7 All creatures of our God and king

4. A Celebration of Animals

(This uses some of the same material as Assembly 3)

Preparation

1. Find a recording of Saint-Saens *Carnival of the Animals* or other music representing animals.

2. Ask the students to write about their feelings for animals, whether pets, wild animals or farm animals, in poetry or prose form.

or

Ask the students to find poems about animals which they find interesting. (Many anthologies include animal poems: a particularly good source is the *Touchstones* series edited by Michael and Peter Benton, published by Hodder and Stoughton.)

or

Help the students prepare a dance or mime based on animal movements, studying videos of the animals if possible.

Assembly

Start with the animal music.

St. Francis of Assisi has been named as the patron saint of ecology, because of his delight in and concern for everything that God has made. He was born in Italy in 1182, and by the end of his life was famous for his preaching of love to all creatures and his life of simplicity and poverty. He addressed animals, plants, fire, stones and water, even death, as his brothers and sisters. He was also known for his sense of fun and his love of music. On one occasion he arrived back in Italy, tired and dispirited because his journey had not achieved what he had hoped. It was dawn, and the place where he landed was filled with the sound of birds chirping and singing. He was delighted to hear the birds, and even more delighted when they did not fly away, but continued singing. He and his companions joined them in singing their morning service. The birds continued singing so loudly that Francis was forced to ask them, "Brother birds, stop singing until we have finished our prayers."

Francis taught that all creatures praise God and have communication with him, and he recognised in them his fellow-worshippers.

Muslims, too, believe that animals, which were created by God, live their lives in praise to God.

Reading

The quotation from the Qur'an on page 24

or

St. Francis' sermon to the birds from page 23-24

or

the verses known as *The Song of Creation* (found in the Anglican Alternative Service Book) or the *Benedicite* (found in the 1662 Book of Common Prayer) or *The song of the Hebrew children* (found in some versions of the Book of Daniel: most accessibly in the Jerusalem Bible as Daniel ch.3, verses 57-90.)

From the *Alternative Service Book*:

1.   Bless the Lord all created things:
      sing his praise and exalt him for ever.

13   O let the earth bless the Lord:
      bless the Lord you mountains and hills;

14   Bless the Lord all that grows in the ground:
      sing his praise and exalt him for ever

15   Bless the Lord you springs:
      bless the Lord you seas and rivers;

16   Bless the Lord you whales and all that swim in the waters:
      sing his praise and exalt him for ever.

17   Bless the Lord all birds of the air:
      bless the Lord you beasts and cattle;

18   Bless the Lord all people on the earth:
      sing his praise and exalt him for ever.

Prayer/reflection

Either use the writing of the students about animals, or the dance they have made up, inviting everyone to give thanks for the richness and variety of animal life.

Hymn

Tell the students that this hymn is based on the song that St. Francis wrote known as the Canticle of the Creatures

Come and Praise
7 All creatures of our God and king

5. Bill of Rights

Preparation
Students prepare to perform one of the plays from Activity 1, page 36
or
Students prepare to present the history of one bill of rights researched in Activity 3, page 36.

Assembly
Start with the presentation the students have prepared (see above)
Then adapt the following to your own style, and to the information presented by the students:

For as far back as history can trace, people have been concerned about the right way to treat each other, and what can be done about it when the rules of right behaviour are broken. In small groups these questions are usually dealt with informally, but as society got more complicated, it became necessary to lay down rules. In different times and in different places, ideas about rights have changed. Sometimes only the wealthy or powerful were thought of as having rights. Sometimes you only had rights if you were born in a particular city, or if you were male.
Sometimes people believed that God had laid down these rights, and they could not be questioned. Sometimes they believed that rights are simply a way to make sure that society does not fall apart. Sometimes they argued that rights could be worked out as a logical process.

The American Declaration of Independence, 1776, was based on what were seen as the basic rights of everyone to 'life, liberty and the pursuit of happiness' - but black slavery was still legal.

In 1948 the United Nations drew up the Universal Declaration of Human Rights:
1. All human beings are born free and equal in dignity and rights...
3. Everyone has the right to life, liberty and security of person.
4. No-one shall be held in slavery or servitude; slavery and the slave trade shall be prohibited in all their forms.
5. No-one shall be subjected to torture or to cruel, inhuman or degrading treatment or punishment.

The extension of the idea of rights to all races, both sexes, to children, animals, and the rest of the natural world, has been a gradual process, not accepted by everyone.

But sometimes people put it a different way round. They argue that instead of talking about rights, we should be thinking about our duties towards others. If everyone fulfiled their duty, they say, there would be no need for rights. Most religious traditions describe people's duties rather than their rights.
But whichever way we think about it, we know there are many people in the world today who are not being treated as they ought to be treated, or who are without the basic means to live their lives in peace and security.

Prayer/reflection

Let us keep silence for a moment and think of some of them. Try to think about a specific person or situation as I suggest different areas:

those who are hungry or have not got clean water to drink;

those who have been falsely imprisoned;

those who live in fear;

those who are forced to work in degrading situations, or those who cannot find work.

What can we do? Let us try in the next few days to think about our duties towards others and how we can help work towards a world where all are able to fulfil their duties towards others.

Hymn

48 Father hear the prayer we offer

50 When a knight won his spurs in the stories of old

65 When I needed a neighbour were you there?

67 The ink is black, the page is white

71 If I had a hammer

73 When your father made the world

74 Sad puzzled eyes

97 'Tis the gift to be simple

6. The Limits of Science

Preparation

Find a re-telling of *The Sorcerers Apprentice*, (originally *Der Zauberlehrling* by Goethe) One good version is retold by Felicity Trotman, published by Methuen Children's Books, London, 1986.

Find a recording of the music, *L'Apprenti Sorcier* by Paul Dukas, and select an appropriate passage; or the soundtrack from Walt Disney's *Fantasia* which uses the same music.

Assembly

Read the story of *The Sorcerer's Apprentice*, or remind the students of it if they are already familiar with it.

Then point out that many people today think of science in the same way that people in the past thought of magic or sorcery: it is done by experts, it can be used for good or bad, and it is very powerful.

Think of some of the benefits we have from:
science
medicine
ease of transport and communication

Think of one technological or scientific advance that you can feel very grateful for.

But scientific discoveries have been used in ways that are not so good, such as:
weapons
providing for people's greed or their competitive instincts.

But it seems that the most common mistake in using scientific knowledge is that, like the apprentice in the story, we make mistakes, or we don't know enough about what we are doing. Nobody knew, when they began to use the insecticide DDT, that it would harm birds as well as killing insects. The inventors of the atom bomb did not know about the effects of nuclear fall-out. Those who began to use animal offal to feed to cattle did not know about the possibility of BSE.

Today we are seeing very powerful advances in genetics and micro-biology. But the results of using them are mixed. Genetic engineering holds out hope of medical advances, and of plants that can help feed the hungry. But it is up to all of us to look carefully at how these discoveries are being used, to ask questions about the results, to ask questions about how much we know. Because there is not always a master-sorcerer to come back, wave his magic wand, and make everything all right again.

Reading

Use the passage quoted from Wisdom on page 58.

Prayer

Ask everyone to remind themselves of the things that they thought of as being good results of science, and to give thanks for them;
then the things they thought of as being bad results, and to reflect on those harmed by them, whether human or animal.

O Lord, give me the strength to change those things I can change;
the patience to accept those things I cannot change;
and the wisdom to know the difference.

Hymn

47 One more step along the world I go
50 When a knight won his spurs

7. The Death of Animals

Preparation

Prepare one or more of the prayers or ceremonies designed by the students in activity 4, page 66–67, for use as a prayer or reflection in the assembly. Prepare to present some of the ideas suggested in activity 4, page 68, for lessening our 'deadly impact' on other animals.

Assembly

All living things die. Mayflies live only one day. Some giant tortoises live for hundreds of years. But eventually everything dies. Many of the stones and rocks of our planet are made up of the skeletons of billions of creatures who died millions of years ago. Many living things die to provide food for other creatures. Flies die in spiders' webs, worms die in the beaks of birds. Mice and voles die in the jaws of cats or the talons of owls and hawks.

Human beings are part of this same natural world. We too die, and many of us eat other creatures.

From earliest times, human beings have recognised that for them to live, other creatures have had to die. In ancient societies such as the traditional people of Canada or Siberia, when an animal is hunted to provide essential food and fur or skins for clothing, ceremonies are performed before and after the hunt asking for forgiveness from the animals. No life is taken lightly.

In Judaism and Islam this idea has been continued. Both have strict laws about how to kill an animal for food. These laws were designed to make the suffering of the animals as short as possible and to ensure that every life taken was dedicated to God as a reminder that God created all life, and no life should be taken lightly. Sadly, today the pressure of numbers in slaughterhouses, whether secular or religious, often means that these principles can get lost.

Even for those of us who do not eat meat, virtually everyone living in Britain has a lifestyle that in some way threatens the life of other creatures: houses and roads destroy animals' habitats; pollution from transport poisons the environment, etc. And yet it seems so difficult to live any other way. Let us reflect on the harm that we do, simply in order to live:

Can we do anything to reduce this harm? Here are some ideas:
Present the students' ideas about doing less harm.

Prayer

Use the ceremony or prayers that the students have prepared.

Reading

When Jesus was preparing for his own death, he compared it to a seed being sown:
John 12:24-25

Hymn

From *Come and Praise*
131 Now the green blade rises

Other Assembly Ideas

If the students are doing more extensive work on the issues raised in this book, there are various ways in which they can present their work and their conclusions to the rest of the school. This would depend on the students' own wishes to present a more 'campaigning' assembly, if a group of them feel strongly. These could include more research and information on, for example, battery egg production, transport of live animals, vegetarianism versus meat-eating.

It is important, however, to make sure that they highlight the implications of their own eating habits, rather than 'pointing the finger' at any other group.

Appendix

Useful addresses

Compassion in World Farming
(CIWF)
5A Charles Street
Petersfield
Hampshire
GU32 3EH

Compassion in World Farming
PO Box 206
Cork
Ireland

Animal Aid
The Old Chapel
Bradford Street
Tonbridge
Kent
TN9 1AW

Advocates for Animals
10 Queensferry Street
Edinburgh
EH2 4PG

Farm Animal Welfare Network
(FAWN)
PO Box 40
Holmfirth
Huddersfield
HD7 1QY

Meat and Livestock Commission
PO Box 44
Milton Keynes
Buckinghamshire
MK6 1AX

National Farmers' Union
22 Long Acre
London
WC2E 9LY

Royal Society for the Prevention of Cruelty to Animals (RSPCA)
Farm Animals Department
Causeway
Horsham
West Sussex
RH12 1HG

Scottish Society for the Prevention of Cruelty to Animals (SSPCA)
Braehead Mains
603 Queensferry Road
Edinburgh
EH3 7PL

The Soil Association (Organic Farming)
86 Colston Street
Bristol
BS1 5BB

World Wide Fund for Animals (WWF)
Panda House
Weyside Park
Godalming
Surrey
GU7 1XR

Vegan Society
7 Battle Road
St Leonards on Sea
East Sussex
TN27 7AA

Vegetarian Society
Parkdale
Dunham Road
Altrincham Cheshire
WA14 4QG

Favourite Animal Survey

Look at the following list of animals and select the three that you like best, in order of preference. Put a score in the box opposite these animals: 5 for your favourite, 3 for second favourite, 1 for third favourite.
It does not matter why you like these animals. Any reason, or no reason, is valid.

dog	☐	cat	☐
sheep	☐	hen	☐
sparrow	☐	panda	☐
tiger	☐	horse	☐
whale	☐	robin	☐
kangaroo	☐	gerbil	☐
pig	☐	mink	☐

- ✂ - - - - - -

Frequency Survey

Put a score in the box according to how frequently you see the following animals, whether live, in pictures, or on television.

more than once a week – 10
about once a week – 9
about once a month – 7
between five and ten times a year – 5
between one and five times a year – 2
less than once a year – 0

dog	☐	cat	☐
sheep	☐	hen	☐
sparrow	☐	panda	☐
tiger	☐	horse	☐
whale	☐	robin	☐
kangaroo	☐	gerbil	☐
pig	☐	mink	☐

Acknowledgments

The preparation of this book has been very much a team effort. In particular we should like to thank Fazlun Khalid and Ranchor Prime of ICOREC, and John Callaghan and Joyce D'Silva of Compassion in World Farming Trust, for the very stimulating working parties which began the project and their advice, enthusiasm and criticism as it progressed. Our colleagues Jo Edwards and Joanne Robinson have also made significant contributions at various stages. Much of our interest and knowledge of this subject arises from work originally supported by World Wide Fund for Nature UK, and many of the quotations we use are from books written by ICOREC and sponsored by WWF. We also owe a debt of gratitude to the late Al-Hafiz B. A. Masri for his pioneering work on the Islamic attitude to animals.

We are grateful for permission to quote copyright material from the following sources:

ICOREC

WWF - Extract from *Faith & Nature*, Nash and Hatting 1987; Extract from *Islam and Ecology*, ed. Khalid and O'Brien 1992; Extract from the *Jain Declaration on Nature.*

Martin Palmer - *Elements of Taoism,* Elements Books, 1991

G.K. Chesterton/A.P. Watt - poem on p.24

Laurence Pollinger Ltd and the Estate of Frieda Lawrence Ravagli - poem on p.46

Complete Poems by Randall Jarrell, published by Faber and Faber Ltd. - poem on p.47

Douglas Adams *The Restaurant at the End of the Universe* published by Pan Books - extract on p.55-56

A Song of Creation is reproduced from *The Alternative Service Book 1980,* © The Central Board of the Church of England

The illustration of the *Hare on the Moon* on p.65 is by Ranchor Prime

Front cover photographs by Robyn Beeche/CIRCA Photolibrary *(top),* and Compassion in World Farming *(bottom)*

Other books from Forbes Publications

Health & Self

The new, fully integrated health education pack for secondary schools

This comprehensive pack provides a health education curriculum for secondary schools and is designed for use with children aged from 12 to 16. The pack contains an Introductory Handbook, three age-related books, each of which contains topic-based units for use in the classroom, and a fourth book on HIV and Aids. Each teaching unit is complete with background notes and a series of photocopiable worksheets.

Contents:
Introductory Handbook for Teachers
Book 1 *(12-14 years)*: • Keeping Safe • Coming of Age • Happy Eating 1 • Health is What You Make It • Facts and Feelings about Drugs and Drug Taking • You in a Group • Smile Please
Book 2 *(14-16 years)*: • Coping with Accidents • Ourselves and Others • Happy Eating 2 • Health and Self • Smoking, Alcohol and Illegal Substances • Lifestyles
Book 3 *(16+ years)*: • Whose Responsibility • Happy Eating 3 • What Help is Available • Skills in Dealing with Drugs Situations • Dilemma
Book 4 *Teaching about HIV and Aids* • Module 1 *(12-14 years)* • Module 2 *(14-16 years)* • Module 3 *(16+ years)*

Health & Self *(pack)*   **Price £54.95**
ISBN 0 901762 85 7
Also available separately:
Introductory Handbook for teachers   **Price £6.95**
ISBN 0 901762 86 5

Available from:
FORBES PUBLICATIONS
3rd floor, Inigo House, 29 Bedford Street London WC2E 9ED
Tel: 0171 379 1299

Science books from Forbes Publications

Science Experiments in Food and Textiles
(3rd edition)
Kevin Howard and Elaine Prisk
The third edition of this popular teaching resource contains over seventy experiments designed for the technology curriculum, focusing on procedures using food and textiles. Each experiment is presented in photocopiable worksheet form and is accompanied by extensive teachers notes, including a new risk assessment component. The GCSE / A level test questions have been revised and expanded and the glossary updated. An essential resource for every science department.
Price £16.95
ISBN 0 901762 97 0

The Science and Technology of Foods
(3rd edition)
R.K. Proudlove
This well established text, now in its third revised edition, meets the needs of students at A level, first year college and NVQ courses. The book includes sections on food composition, commodities and raw materials, handling and preservation of food, and raw materials and preservation. An excellent and practical teaching resource.
Price £16.50
ISBN 0 901762 62 8

Technology of Textile Properties
(3rd edition)
Marjorie A. Taylor
This best-selling, hugely popular textbook is tailored for textile studies at A level and in further and higher education. Constantly updated, the third edition is an excellent introduction to the world of textiles and is used in many textile courses throughout the UK.
Price £16.50
ISBN 0 901762 82 2

Available from:
FORBES PUBLICATIONS
3rd floor, Inigo House, 29 Bedford Street London WC2E 9ED
Tel: 0171 379 1299